What Primary Teachers
should know about
ASSESSMENT

PRIMARY BOOKSHELF

What Primary Teachers should know about ASSESSMENT

Aileen Duncan and William Dunn

Hodder & Stoughton
LONDON SYDNEY AUCKLAND

ISBN 0 340 40830 8

Copyright © 1988 Aileen Duncan and William Dunn
First published 1988
Fifth impression 1991
Sixth impression 1992

Typeset by Wessex Typesetters
(Division of The Eastern Press Ltd)
Frome, Somerset.

Printed and bound in Great Britain for
Hodder and Stoughton Educational,
a division of Hodder and Stoughton Ltd,
Mill Road, Dunton Green, Sevenoaks, Kent,
by Thomson Litho Ltd, East Kilbride, Scotland.

Contents

Introduction

This book is concerned with decisions made by individual teachers in the classroom. The focus of the book is on assessment techniques, and it will help teachers to consider the language of assessment. It has been written as a contribution to the continuing education of teachers.

This book is not the definitive textbook containing all there is to know about assessment in the primary school – there is no point in that within a continuing education programme. Rather, the book is based on the following assumptions:

- Primary school teachers already know quite a lot about assessment.
- Perhaps the majority of primary school teachers do not want or expect to be experts on assessment; thus the traditional textbooks on assessment are not much use to them! In our experience what most primary teachers are looking for is some indication of what it is reasonable to expect them to know in order to make a reasonable job of their classroom practice.
- The primary teacher wants to find out what he or she does not know and needs to know, and to be pointed in the right direction to do something about it.

The book is based on practical ideas and it attempts to provide practical guidelines. The ideas contained in it are set out as succinctly as possible. It was used as part of the national course, Assessment in the Primary School, which was sponsored by the Scottish Education Department and organised by the Inservice Department of Jordanhill College of Education.

The authors were unsuccessful in their search for a suitable text which was designed as a reference book for primary teachers. Most standard texts on assessment are intended for secondary school work and for external examinations. So this book was written. It does not claim to be comprehensive but merely to outline what, in the authors' judgement, every primary teacher should know.

Throughout the book, year-groups are identified using the Scottish terminology P1, P2 . . . P7. Years P1 and P2 correspond to the English Infants stage, and P3 to P7 to the Junior stage (the Scottish system having an additional year of primary education).

1 Assessment, evaluation and the curriculum

The terms 'assessment' and 'evaluation' are often confused. Rather than pursue what each term can and cannot mean, we have given a working definition of each. These working definitions highlight the distinction between the two terms.

Assessment is the process of gathering information

- by teachers about their pupils;
- by teachers about their teaching; and
- by pupils about their progress.

Current practice in the primary school places most emphasis on the first activity. However, there is an increasing emphasis on the second and an awareness of the third.

Evaluation is always present when teachers do their work. It involves making judgements, which can be based on the information provided by the processes of assessment. This is preferable to basing judgements solely on impression – a much less systematic way of gathering information.

Assessment involves decisions about techniques and procedures, and is always secondary to some more important considerations which have to do with

- the curriculum;
- the pupil; or
- both.

These considerations are the focus of evaluation.

Teachers can agree about the method of gathering information, the assessment process. There is less agreement, however, among teachers about the evaluation drawn from the assessment information. There are two sources for the disagreement:

1 different philosophical conceptions of the primary school curriculum, the learning process and the nature of the child;
2 different perceptions of the process of information gathering – the assessment process.

This book aims to explore the latter and find common ground.

In primary schools there is increasing emphasis on curriculum. HM Inspectorate has been encouraging schools to do more than merely assess individual subjects. Schools are being asked to assess their curriculum, as well as continuing to assess subjects. They want headteachers to take greater responsibility for the management of the curriculum, and this involves assessing whether or not curricular aims are being progressed.

What do we mean by the curriculum? Two aspects should receive prominence in any description: first, that learning should follow a clearly defined sequence, and, second, that it should form a rounded whole. The curriculum should be rather more than the sum of its parts. It derives its educational power as much from the bonding of its parts as it does from the internal characteristics of the parts themselves. In these terms, the curriculum is more than a cluster of educational topics, just as a house is more than a pile of bricks. (A list of topics is better described as a syllabus.)

It follows that any system of assessment should be able to accommodate

1 the elements of the curriculum – that is, the individual subjects; and
2 the curriculum as a whole.

The system we propose does this. We call it an 'across-the-curriculum' approach.

For example, if you want to assess a child's performance in mathematics, you have to decide what aspect of the child's ability you wish to gather information about. You might want to know if the child can carry out an addition calculation. We would classify this in the 'across-the-curriculum' approach as 'acquisition of knowledge'.

In mathematics, however, you might present a child with a question like the following: 'Find a number that divides exactly by all the numbers one to ten. Explain if this is the only number that is suitable.' Here you might want to know if the child can interpret instructions, realise which concepts and principles have to be applied, and be able to apply them. We would classify this as 'problem solving'.

In the same way, if you wish to assess a child's performance in religious education, you would consider the aspect to assess and discover if the same classification, which we have just considered for mathematics, is suitable. For example, a question which illustrates 'acquisition of knowledge' could be: 'Who led the Israelites out of Egypt?', and a question for the 'problem solving' aspect could be: 'Choose a Bible reading and a hymn about the harvest.'

The classification we propose could be thought of as another way of looking at the curriculum. The classification focuses on what the child knows and can do, rather than on the subject matter. We shall explain the categories of the classification in detail, and, as you read, you should be able to relate these more clearly to different subjects. However, in Chapter 4 there are assessment examples where the subject link is made more explicit.

2 A classification for assessment

The classification we suggest is as follows:

1 the acquisition of knowledge, of concepts, of principles;
2 the ability to apply concepts and principles to new situations;
3 the ability to communicate;
4 the ability to solve problems (something more than the ability to apply knowledge to new situations); and
5 attitudes.

For each of these five separate categories we answer the following questions:

- What do we mean?
- Why assess it?
- Whom do you assess?
- What do you assess?
- How do you assess it?
- When is it appropriate to assess it?
- How do you record or retain the information arising from the assessment?
- Who gets this information?
- How should the assessment information be evaluated?

Throughout this section you will find terms in bold-face print. Each of these is explained in Chapter 5.

The acquisition of knowledge

What do we mean?

By the acquisition of knowledge we mean that the child knows:

> specific facts, terminology, classifications, criteria, methods (knowing how to do it, but not necessarily able to do it), concepts and principles (knowledge of the concept or principle, but not necessarily an ability to apply it).

Acquisition of knowledge is a necessary first step in any educational process. There may be debate about the selection of knowledge, but there is no question that knowledge is necessary, and that its acquisition should be assessed as part of good teaching practice.

Why assess the acquisition of knowledge?

You assess for **formative** purposes to find out whether or not a child needs knowledge to be taught or has acquired the knowledge recently taught. The acquisition of the necessary knowledge is the first step towards the acquisition of **concepts** and **principles**.

Whom do you assess?

The teacher wants to assess whether or not the individual pupil has acquired a piece of knowledge. Each individual may be assessed as part of the class or a group as a classroom-management strategy, but the focus of assessment is the individual.

What do you assess?

The teacher tests the recall of specific facts, classification and so on, but also assesses the ability to translate the presented material into a more meaningful form – the ability to interpret and comprehend. The teacher must choose or devise a test item which **validly** tests the knowledge.

Assessment of the acquisition of knowledge can be a laborious affair; theoretically, each acquisition has to be tested, item by item. We can reduce the laboriousness by sampling the content, but that can lead to misleading information for the teacher because the sampling can be poorly chosen. We can increase the **reliability** of a test of the acquisition of knowledge of a given subject or topic by increasing the number of test items.

How do you assess the acquisition of knowledge?

Technique	Comment
Multiple choice questions (MCQs)	MCQs are more frequently tests of verbal reasoning than of the acquisition of knowledge. Pupils are heavily prompted through the choices. It is difficult to select **valid** items and probably is not worth the effort. However, because MCQs can be answered quickly, more questions can be asked and the field of knowledge can thus be better sampled.
Completion items	Completion items are easier to make up than MCQs. The difficulty is that they frequently contain **formal prompts** which can serve to misprompt and mislead.
Answering questions	Answering direct questions on paper, orally or by demonstration, is the best test of the acquisition of knowledge.
Writing	Extended writing should test much more than the acquisition of knowledge. It is usually difficult to separate the knowledge component from the other components. It can be done, but it needs to be done systematically, with a separate score for each component.
Assessment activities	These also test much more than the acquisition of knowledge.
Structured observation and listening	Structured observation and listening is seldom used for the acquisition of knowledge.
Informal assessment	Informal assessment is not nearly systematic enough to assess the acquisition of knowledge.

We suggest that you select questions from textbooks, adapt them or make up your own. You can also use the following framework of verbs and objects for your questions:

Examples of infinitives	Examples of direct objects
to define, to distinguish, to identify, to recall, to recognise	vocabulary, meaning, facts, rules, symbols, processes, influences, methods
to translate, to give in own words, to prepare, to read, to change, to interpret, to explain, to fill in, to draw	meanings, conclusions, methods, consequences, implications

To illustrate how this framework can be used, let us consider, for example, the verb 'to identify' and the object 'vocabulary'. A question for the objective 'to identify vocabulary' could be 'Find one word which means that an event happens every day'. Another example from the framework could be 'to translate implications'. Children might be asked: 'Look at the clockwork car moving across the wooden floor. What would happen if it was placed on the carpet?'

When is it appropriate to assess the acquisition of knowledge?

Assessment of the acquisition of knowledge is usually built into the teaching situation. Its purpose is formative, to help the teacher decide what to do next.

Appropriate times for the assessment of the acquisition of knowledge would be:

- at the beginning or end of a topic,
- at the beginning or end of a term,
- at the beginning or end of a session,

but mainly as an ongoing part of classwork.

How do you record or retain the information arising from the assessment?

With one or two exceptions, it is not necessary to record the acquisition of knowledge. In the past, this aspect of assessment was considered important, and marks and grades were based solely on the learner's mastery of facts.

Acquisition of knowledge is the first stage in developing concepts and principles. It is also the first stage of the rational development of **attitudes**. It is the later stages which are recorded. If these later stages are mastered successfully, it is assumed that the necessary acquisition of knowledge has taken place.

One exception to this rule is **diagnostic** assessment in remedial situations, where a teacher or remedial specialist might set out to determine whether or not a child had acquired the necessary knowledge to develop a concept or principle.

Who gets this information?

Assessment of the acquisition of knowledge is usually undertaken by the teacher for formative purposes. Rarely need the information be passed on.

How do you evaluate the assessment information?

It is difficult to generalise from a sample of items; a child may score highly on a sample of test items which test the acquisition of knowledge in a particular field but still have major gaps in essential knowledge. This reflects the 'sample error' – the fact that so few items are chosen to represent such a wide field. The larger the sample of items in the field the more **reliable** the measures become.

Acquisition of knowledge is usually assessed indirectly through assessment of concepts and principles. If a child uses a concept correctly, it is assumed that he or she has acquired the necessary knowledge. The error is to regard the acquisition of knowledge as something worthwhile in itself.

The ability to apply concepts and principles

What do we mean?

A child can possess knowledge of a concept or principle but be unable to apply it. Here we are referring to the situation in which a child is using his or her understanding of a concept or principle in a context which may be unfamiliar to him. In the curriculum, the concepts and principles might be from mathematics, environmental studies, English or science.

It is important to distinguish between the assessment which aims to ascertain whether a concept or principle has been comprehended, and that which aims to quantify an ability to apply this concept or principle to a specific situation. For example, children may have grasped the concept of an even number for the range of numbers 1 to 20, but they may not be able to apply this concept to a number such as 2314.

Why assess the ability to apply concepts and principles?

The case for the application of concepts and principles to concrete situations is self-evident. The common fault is that we delude ourselves that we are applying concepts and principles when in fact all we are doing is assessing the recall of knowledge and comprehension. For example, look at this question:

'Which of these shapes is a kite?'

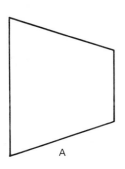 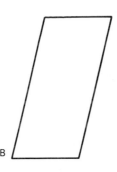 

The child could answer C by recalling a previous example. However, the following question is more demanding and requires the child to consider his concept of a kite:

'One of these shapes is not a kite. Which is it?'

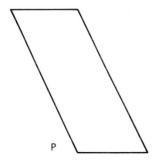 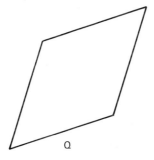 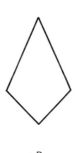 

Whom do you assess?

You will want to assess whether or not the individual child has acquired the ability to apply the concept or principle to a specific situation. You may assess the individual as part of the class or in a group situation as a classroom-management strategy.

What do you assess?

You want to assess whether or not the child can apply concepts and principles. In the primary school there are two pitfalls:

1 We test the recall of knowledge and comprehension of the concept rather than the ability to apply it to specific situations.

2 When we use written methods of assessment, the **validity** of the test item may be questioned because of the difficulties of language. There are two difficulties:

(a) the specific situation has to be described to the child, so there is the difficulty of ensuring that the child understands the description;

(b) there are many situations where the child can apply a concept or principle but is unable to describe what he or she has done, especially in written form.

How do you assess the application of concepts and principles?

Technique	Comment
Multiple choice questions (MCQs)	MCQs are more frequently tests of verbal reasoning than applications of concepts and principles. Children are heavily prompted through the choices. It is difficult to construct valid items. Most examples that we have seen ask for one correct answer from a choice of four or one correct answer from a choice of five. MCQs and matching questions which do assess the ability to apply concepts and principles are usually long.
Completion items	Completion items are easier to make up than MCQs. Completion items usually assess recall of knowledge or comprehension; rarely do they test the application of knowledge. In practice, written questions testing written application of concepts and principles have to be quite long. The question has to assess the ability to apply a concept or a principle to a specific situation, and the specific situation takes some time to describe!
Answering direct questions	Answering direct questions on paper, orally or by demonstration, is an important way of testing the ability to apply concepts or principles to specific situations. Again, the problem is that the questions are not brief – they have to describe the specific situation.
	Many mathematics questions claim to assess the application of concepts and rules but mainly in fact test comprehension.
Writing	Writing usually tests much more than the acquisition of knowledge and, indeed, application of knowledge to specific situations. However, very often the emphasis is wrong. There is a short question from the teacher and a long answer from the child. In the application of concepts and principles the emphasis should be on a rather detailed description of specific situations. The question is long; usually the answer required of the child can be quite brief.
Assessment activities	Since application is concerned with the application of concepts and principles to specific situations, very often the most valid way of proceeding is to provide the child with the practical situation and observe how the concepts and principles are applied: for example, 'Put 200 g of rice in the bag'.
Structured observation and listening	Observing and listening is an ideal way to assess a child's ability to apply a concept or principle if the teacher wishes to help the child overcome learning difficulties. For example, for the weighing task mentioned in the assessment activity section, the teacher can find out if a child is

unable to make up the bag correctly. However, if the child is observed weighing the bag, the teacher may be able to find out what difficulties the child is experiencing.

If you are using questions from textbooks, adapt them for your own teaching situation. If you make up your own questions, use the following framework:

Examples of infinitives	*Examples of direct objects*
to apply, to generalise, to relate, to choose, to develop, to organise, to use, to employ, to transfer, to restructure, to classify.	principles, laws, conclusions, methods, generalisations, processes, procedures.

For example, if you would like to find out if the children can 'develop a method', you could ask them: 'Write out rules to tell you what to do when you want to write a word and can't spell it.'

When do you assess the application of concepts and principles?

Assessment of the application of concepts and principles is usefully built into the teaching situation. Structured observation of the children in specific situations can confirm either that they can apply a concept or it will give some indication of the nature of their difficulty. This is **formative** assessment.

Assessment of the application of concepts and principles should also take place as part of **summative** assessment

- at the end of a topic, and/or
- at the end of a term, and/or
- at the end of a session.

How do you record or retain the information arising from the assessment?

It is worthwhile recording which concepts or principles a child can apply. This might be done in the child's profile, listing the important concepts and principles which the child has successfully applied in a number of specific situations.

Who gets this information?

This is the sort of information that you need to know in order to plan further teaching. Remember that assessment is a necessary part of the teaching/learning cycle; it will tell you what elements of your teaching the child has learned well enough to be able to apply them. It is also well worth passing on to the next teacher, and to the secondary school.

This is also information which you should pass on to the child and to the parents. Care needs to be taken with the language used so as to make the information meaningful.

How do you evaluate this information?

A decision has to be made as to the range of specific situations in which the child must demonstrate application of concepts or principles, in order to be satisfied that the child can carry this application through in all situations. The range of specific situations to be chosen is a matter of professional judgement.

Communication

What do we mean?

In the context of the curriculum in the primary

school, both formal and informal, communication by a child implies:

- the acquisition of knowledge and of concepts and principles;
- the ability to apply these concepts and principles to specific situations;
- the breaking down of elements in the presented material and the recognition of relationships and organisation of the whole; and
- the synthesising of elements or parts to form a whole, which is then communicated.

    This communication can be:

- in writing;
- in oral form; or
- by gesture and 'body language'.

Why assess the ability to communicate?

There are certain elements of communication which receive emphasis in the primary school. They are as follows:

1 written communication –
    creative writing,
    poetry,
    interpretation,
    writing answers to questions;
2 reading –
    reading out loud to the teacher,
    reading silently for understanding.

There is much less emphasis on assessment of oral communication between the child and the teacher, and between children, yet in the outside world oral communication is so important. Nobody would claim that the primary school had neglected to promote oral communication, but perhaps it has been less than systematic in assessing progress in this direction.

Whom do you assess?

For oral communication, it is the individual child who is assessed. The assessment is likely to involve a tape recorder where the child is giving an oral answer or listening to a recorded voice or voices. The child's ability to talk to and listen to others in a small group situation should of course also be assessed.

What do you assess?

You will want to know if the child can do the following things:

1 talk to another child;
2 talk informally to the teacher;
3 talk to the rest of the class;
4 produce a tape-recorded report;
5 write a simple account;
6 write an evaluative report;
7 write poetry;
8 write creatively;
9 draw or paint to express ideas or feelings connected with the topic;
10 draw a graph;
11 construct a map;
12 make models;
13 take a photograph;
14 make a video tape;
15 compose music;
16 make a visual display;
17 make an audio-visual display.

The child usually knows his strengths and weaknesses in methods of communication, and is prepared to

- improve his skills and methods of communication, particularly those in which he is relatively weak;
- choose a method of communication appropriate to the message;
- choose a method of communication which is appropriate to the intended receiver.

    The following are examples of assessment questions.

1 Tell John how to get from school to your house.
2 Write the rules for your game.
3 Make up a dance which tells a story.
4 Draw a graph to show the number of vehicles passing school at lunchtime.

How do you assess the ability to communicate?

Formal methods of assessment are not always appropriate for the assessment of communication. Very often communication can be observed in informal situations. The reliability of the observations can be increased through the use of a checklist. In a comment on a child, reference to a checklist is much better than a personal opinion.

Here is some help for constructing a checklist to assess communication:

1 the subject for communication should be a concrete situation;
2 the aspects of communication to be assessed should be clearly identified and possibly grouped;
3 use a Yes/No or Satisfactory/Unsatisfactory answer for each item – any compromise may introduce complications at the evaluation stage.

When using a checklist:

1 only attempt to observe one or two children at a time;
2 it is important to provide feedback to children – is there any reason why they should not see your checklist?

When do you assess the ability to communicate?

Much communication can be assessed in the classroom during normal teaching situations. This can provide useful feedback to the teacher. Our suggestion is to go one step further and try to build the assessment of communication into the activity you have designed for the child or the group of children. Such assessment is **formative**. For example:

1 Do children understand a question they have been given? Ask them to tell you on tape in their own words what it means.
2 Check that a child can tell you how he carries out a calculation.

There can be more complete assessment of communication at the end of a term or a year. Here we suggest structured assessment activities, for example:

1 Write an invitation to a party. Address the envelope too.
2 Tell William, the new boy to the class, how to go from our classroom to the headteacher's room.

How do you record or retain this information?

Checklists should not be seen as an end in themselves. They should be designed to allow the teacher to tick or make short comments. These should be the basis of a few sentences on each child's performance, focusing on individual strengths and weaknesses. This report will be part of a child's overall profile.

It would also be effective to have a tape for each individual child in order to keep a record of his or her fluency when describing, reporting and giving opinions.

Who gets this information?

You need this information for future teaching. The child, the parent and colleagues in education will also benefit from knowing strengths and weaknesses in communication.

11

How do you evaluate this information?

We advise emphasising the **validity** of the assessment technique, even if this has to be at the expense of **reliability**. The use of a checklist during oral assessment improves reliability.

With both written and oral communication, holistic assessment (sometimes called 'impression marking') can be useful, but the grave danger is that it can tell more about the assessor than the assessed, and omissions in the content can be ignored because of familiarity and/or the **halo effect**.

Problem solving

What do we mean?

Surely the major reason for learning to apply concepts and principles is in order to use them to solve problems. Problem solving is the rational extension of applying concepts and principles. The main difference between the application of concepts and principles and problem solving is that when a child attempts to solve a problem he has to determine for himself which concepts and/or principles are to be applied and then use these to find the solution. When the particular combination of rules that fit the situation are found and used, the child has not only solved the problem but has also learned something new. So problem solving is more than simply using the rules to achieve some goal; in the process something is learned which changes the child's capability. The solution becomes part of the child's repertoire; the same situation, when encountered again, may be met with greater facility by means of recall.

Problem solving differs from rule learning in the amount of guidance given to the child. In rule learning the questions cue the solutions (this is true of many examples in mathematics). Problem solving draws on the child's learning and experiences from across the curriculum and also from life.

It is worthwhile distinguishing between a 'problem' and 'difficulty'. We have difficulty learning people's names but rarely is this a problem – rarely does it lead to any learning on our part!

Why assess the ability to solve problems?

There is today increased concern about inert ideas. These are ideas which are only useful in school to pass the school examinations and for assessments by teachers; they have little relevance in the outside world. This situation arises because emphasis is placed on the assessment of the acquisition of knowledge.

Increasingly, curricular intentions reflect an emphasis on concepts and principles and an ability to use these in new situations. In the statements of these intentions there is growing emphasis on problem solving, and, if this is important enough to be stated in the curriculum itself, then it is important enough to be assessed.

Most of us would acknowledge our limited insight into how children solve problems. Our first objectives in assessing problem solving, therefore, might simply be to gain more insight into this process ourselves.

Whom do you assess?

If a child is working with others to solve a problem, he is encouraged to make his ideas, opinions and modifications of ideas more explicit. So while it is the individual who is assessed, in the primary school this is best carried out when the child is working with others. This is where you are most likely to find out the steps an individual takes towards a solution because he or she has to make these clear to the others and to convince them that this is what the group should do.

It is, however, possible to give the individual the opportunity to talk about, write about or demonstrate his or her own solution to a given problem.

What do you assess?

Problem solving is more than using rules to achieve some goal: in the processing something has to be learned which changes the child's capability. The same situation, when encountered again, will be recalled, and this is the basic practical difficulty for the teacher: to present children with problems to be solved

- where they have not met the situation before;
- where they have the necessary concepts and principles to find a solution; or
- where they can learn the necessary concepts and rules as they work towards a solution.

A teacher needs a considerable supply of problems devised for specific age groups. Children are interested in real life problems and they are interested in solutions to these problems. Yet the curriculum is divided into disciplines, forms of knowledge that do not relate easily to the outside world.

It is difficult (but not impossible) to devise problems for children within disciplines. It is much easier to devise problems which cut across boundaries within the curriculum. In the primary school most problems should be practical. Here are some examples, taken from a project funded by the Scottish Education Department entitled 'Problem solving in the primary school', now published by Ginn as the series *We've Done It*:

Nursery/P1 Make a tower taller than anyone in the class.
Materials: enough large plastic bricks for *one* tall tower.
P2/P3 Make a garage for the car. Drive the car into it when you are ready.
Materials: sheet of A4 card, scissors, glue or Sellotape.

P4/5 Make up a jingle about keeping the school tidy.
Use the glockenspiel.
When you are ready, teach the jingle to a classmate.
Materials: glockenspiel.
P6/7 Make up a game for three players where the same player is always the winner.
Try it out.
Materials: children's own choice.

What you would assess is *not* the children's ability to find a solution but their process towards finding one. For example, does the child

- take time to consider a plan of action,
- listen to the answers,
- have suggestions about what to do, and make these suggestions explicit,
- make constructive comments,
- adapt a suggestion, and
- ask questions . . . and so on.

How do you assess the ability to solve problems?

Recent research work in the primary school suggests that children can solve problems effectively by working in small groups. You might want to assess the ability of an individual child to participate in a group of peers to solve a problem. This would involve observing the group of children, using a checklist of the behaviours you wish to assess. (Some suggested behaviours are listed in the previous section.) The coding used in the checklist should later be the basis of a statement about the child's ability for his or her profile.

If the objective is to find out if the individual child has learned from problem-solving sessions, then the technique is to provide children with a similar problem to be solved where each is working individually and has a limited time to solve the problem.

Those children who have learned from their problem-solving experiences will recall

13

what they have learned, and use this knowledge to solve the problem. Those who have not learned will have to attempt the problem from scratch, and this will take very much longer.

strated by the individual child's ability to find solutions quickly. The classes of problems should be derived from the curricular aims and objectives. Those that have been mastered should be recorded for each child.

When do you assess the problem-solving ability?

If you want to assess the ability of an individual child to participate in a group of peers to solve a problem, then the appropriate time to do this is when the children are working together. Make notes, or mark the checklist whenever you have the opportunity. This means that assessment will be intermittent and will be used as a basis for teaching (formative assessment). The teaching should be part of the developmental programme for problem solving.

If you want to assess whether or not children have learned from the problem-solving experiences, then assessments would be at the end of a topic, a term, or a session (summative assessment).

Who gets this information?

Information on the assessment of problem-solving behaviours and classes of problems solved is very important information for you in order that you may plan for the child's progress in this relatively new field of learning. It is also important to the next teacher in the primary school or in the secondary school.

This information should be made available to the child and the parents, but again the language used to convey the child's progress must be meaningful to them. It is also important for the curriculum developers – there isn't enough systematic feedback to the developers.

How do you record or retain the information acquired?

It is important to record whether or not the child has acquired the following capabilities:

1 to understand the problem;
2 to suggest possible methods for its solution;
3 to try out one or two methods to achieve a solution;
4 to evaluate the solution in terms of the given problem and of the group's or the child's own performance.

For each child it is also important to record the classes of problems which are, in effect, no longer problems for that child, as demon-

How do you evaluate this information?

The teacher should be interested to find out if the child

1 is making progress in communication and social skills when interacting in the group,
2 is extending his methods of approach, modification and so on in order to solve problems, and
3 when presented with a problem which can be solved in a similar way to one he has already met, realises this similarity.

The teacher will also gain a great deal of feedback on children's creativity, ingenuity and persuasiveness in presenting their viewpoints.

Attitude

What do we mean?

In the assessment of the acquisition of knowledge, the application of concepts and principles to specific situations, and problem solving, we assess *what the child is able to do.* When
we assess attitudes, we assess, from all the
things that a child is able to do, *what the child
chooses to do.* And what the child chooses to do
is a reflection of his or her attitude.

Why assess attitude?

Most teachers have always believed that what
they do now will affect and influence children's behaviour in the future; in other words,
they have influenced children's attitudes.
The trend now is that we should be more
systematic about it.

Most sets of curricular aims include statements about attitudes. In many cases – and
this is perhaps more true in the secondary
school than in the primary school – the
assessment of attitudes is given very low
priority indeed. And if attitudes are not important enough to assess, then neither children
nor teachers will take curricular attitudes
seriously.

Why are attitudes not assessed? There is
concern that assessment smacks of a 'big
brother state'. But we do know that curricular
aims do reflect attitudes, and if we do attempt
to teach them surely we should try to assess
them? Our concerns are the attitudes reflected
in curricular aims and objectives.

Many teachers think that attitudes can be
assessed by questionnaire. There is, rightly,
concern about the validity and reliability of the
questionnaire technique. However, observational techniques can take us quite a long way
in avoiding the disadvantages associated with
questionnaires.

Whom do you assess?

Usually we want to assess the attitude of the
individual child. But there are times when we
want to assess the attitude of the class as a
whole, and, at other times, of the whole
school.

The authors recall one nursery teacher
being praised because of the very caring
attitude that the class had towards a little blind
girl who was one of their number. And they
also recall an HMI saying that he could
quickly detect the ethos of the school (reflect-
ing the attitudes both of children and staff),
and that he spent the rest of the day, or days,
looking for reasons to support the conclusion
he had already reached. In one case the
attitude of the class had been assessed, and in
the second the attitude of the school.

What do you assess?

Attitudes reflect what a child chooses to do
(from all the things that he or she is able to do).
So the assessment of the situation must
involve choice. Once you start to think about
it, it is relatively straightforward to decide
whether or not a child has the attitude that you
seek to inculcate.

Your problem is assessing the progress that
individual children are making towards the
development of particular attitudes – you
know that the child doesn't have the attitude
you want, and wonder whether you are making
any progress towards shaping it. It is useful to
recognise the following stages; they were
originally published in Krathwohl *et al.* (1964)
but are more commonly known as Bloom's
Taxonomy in the Affective Domain.

Receiving

At this level we are concerned that the child is
willing to receive or to attend. This is clearly
the first and crucial step if the learner is to be

properly oriented to learn what the teacher would like him to learn. For example,

attends (carefully) when others speak, when working in a group, when being taught by the teacher;
shows tolerance of children who are different from themselves in dress, appearance, home, manners, beliefs.

Responding

At this level we are concerned with responses which go beyond merely attending to the phenomenon. The child is sufficiently motivated that he is not just *willing to attend* but is *actively attending.*

This is the category that many teachers will find best describes their 'interest' objectives. For example, the child will show an interest in the collection of leaves. Most commonly we use the term to indicate that a child becomes sufficiently involved in or committed to a subject or activity that he will seek it out and gain satisfaction from engaging in it.

Further examples are when a child shows the following responses:

- acceptance of responsibility by cleaning out the cage of the class guinea pig and feeding it;
- pleasure in reading for recreation; or
- enjoyment in playing the recorder.

Valuing

This is the only category headed by a term which is in common use in the expression of objectives by teachers. Further, it is employed in its usual sense: that a thing, phenomenon or behaviour has worth. This abstract concept of worth is in part a result of the individual's own valuing or assessment, but it is much more a social product that has been slowly internalised or accepted and has come to be used by the child as his own criterion of worth.

This category will be found appropriate for

many objectives that use the term 'attitude' (as well as, of course, 'value'); for example, 'The child will have the correct attitude to the music'.

An important element of behaviour characterised by valuing is that it is motivated not by the desire to comply or obey, but by the individual's commitment to the underlying value guiding the behaviour. For example, think why you obey the parking regulations. Do you obey because the traffic wardens might come around (responding)? Or do you obey whether there are traffic wardens or not (valuing)?

Organisation

As the child successively internalises values, he encounters situations for which more than one value is relevant. Thus necessity arises for

1 organisation of the values into a system,
2 the determination of the interrelationships among them, and
3 the establishment of the dominant and pervasive ones.

For example, a child carries messages for an elderly neighbour not just once but every Saturday morning over a long period of time, while continuing to play in the school football team.

Characterisation by a value or value complex

The individual acts consistently in accordance with the values he has internalised. For example, the child is litter-conscious in the classroom, the playground, at home and in the street. Such actions are normally associated with post-school behaviour. They are what we aspire to in curricular terms. We are unlikely to be able to assess them in school, but we get glimpses of them when the children are on a visit out of school, particularly when the teacher is not present.

How do you assess attitude?

Technique	Comment
Multiple choice questions (MCQs)	Surprisingly, MCQs are often used to assess attitudes. Have you ever tried any of the self-assessment quizzes in magazines like *Cosmopolitan*? You make your choice, turn to another page, mark your choice and develop a score which reflects your attitude. But the choices are **prompted**!
Completion items (answering questions)	Questionnaires, which often depend on completion items are of doubtful validity, particularly for children in primary schools. You may have seen the episode of 'Yes, Prime Minister' in which the Secretary to the Cabinet explained to the Prime Minister how it was possible to design two questionnaires; one of these would show support in the nation for the reintroduction of National Service, and the other would show support for the rejection of its reintroduction. The difference was simply in the way and the order in which the questions were asked. Educational psychologists use questionnaires in their assessments, but these questionnaires have been extensively piloted and norms are available. The interpretation of the data is fairly sophisticated. There are a number of **published tests** of attitudes available.
Writing	Written work can reflect some attitudes, but it depends very much on circumstances and the children's ability to express themselves. Primary children do tend to reveal attitudes in their writing, but infrequently attitudes related to curricular intentions. You cannot count on assessing curricular attitudes consistently through writing.
Assessment activities	Certain types of attitude can be assessed in a practical situation – for example, attitudes towards use of equipment. A P4 child can choose to use centimetre cubes or a ruler to find the length of a pencil. The choice may reflect the child's value (or confidence) in using a ruler.
Structured observation and listening	There is little doubt that observing children, especially as they change from one lesson to another and as they move from one activity, or class, to another, as well as in the playground, is most revealing about attitudes. However, it does mean deciding in advance on behaviours which indicate the attitude for which you are looking.
Informality	The informal situation should be the main focus when you are looking for attitudinal factors. As far as the child is concerned, the situation should be unstructured or semi-structured, so he has plenty of choice. We suggest that attitudes can be assessed in the informal or practical situations using your own checklist, based on your own curriculum.

Overleaf is a framework which will help you construct statements at the various attitudinal levels.

Since the assessment of attitudes is best done in informal situations, it is important to be systematic in your coverage of the children in your class, and only attempt to observe one or two children at one time (unless you have eyes in the back of your head). This means that the assessment of attitudes tends to be spread out in an on-going activity. The various assessments throughout the year, of course, should be consolidated in a final report.

Examples of infinitives	Examples of direct objects
1 *Receiving* to accumulate, to select, to combine, to accept.	models, examples, shapes.
2 *Responding* to comply (with), to follow, to commend, to approve.	directions, instructions, policies, demonstrations.
to volunteer, to discuss, to practise, to play.	instruments, games, works, charades.
3 *Valuing* to increase measured proficiency in, to increase numbers of, to specify.	group membership(s), artistic production, personal friendships.
to assist, to help, to support.	projects, viewpoints, arguments.
to deny, to protest, to debate, to argue.	deceptions, irrelevances, irrationalities.
4 *Organisation* to discuss, to theorise (on), to abstract, to compare.	parameters, codes, standards, goals.
to balance, to organise, to define, to formulate.	systems, approaches, criteria, limits.

How do you record or retain the information?

Information has to be recorded in order to be retained. Our impressions and our memories are simply not reliable enough about most children. It is worthwhile recording the attitudes you wish to promote. Prepare a checklist of actions which you can observe and which would reflect progress in attitude. This checklist becomes the basis of any report you write. Assessment of attitudes should be part of summative assessment.

Who gets this information?

As the attitudes to be monitored may be part of school policy, other teachers would wish to have the information.

Where comment on a child's attitude is made to parents, you should have evidence to support this. Too often a report is written, stating (for example), 'is not interested', without any objective evidence.

How do you evaluate this information?

Do you feel uncomfortable with assessment of attitudes? Do you feel it smacks of 'big brother'? Three points follow which may allay your fears:

1 Do you believe that what we do now in the classroom will affect the child's choice of action in the future? The answer is surely 'yes'; teachers are already in the business of shaping attitudes.
2 In this book we are concerned with the attitudinal statements in curricular aims and objectives. We are not concerned with the unstated aims and objectives of the hidden curriculum which are unchallenged but which are assessed and reported. (The evidence for this lies in children's reports from any school.)
3 If we assess stages in development of attitudes, we can begin to think of strategies of promoting the attitude changes we seek.

We must use a conceptual structure for our assessments. We have all read assessments of attitudes of children that depended on impression. Such attitudes tell you much more about the assessor than the assessed. An example of an assessment based on impression is the following: 'David doesn't show an interest in practical work in mathematics.' If we depend on impression, the reports on attitudes can tell us much more about the teacher than the class, due to the **halo effect.**

3 The techniques of assessment

There are eight techniques of assessment which are relevant to the primary school. You have already met these in Chapter 2. They are:

1 multiple choice questions and matching questions;
2 sentence completion;
3 answering direct questions;
4 extended writing;
5 assessment activities;
6 structured observation and listening;
7 informal assessment; and
8 published tests and inventories.

For each of these techniques, we shall explain

- what we mean;
- examples of good practice;
- the advantages claimed for the technique;
- practical hints on use; and
- evaluation of the information which arises.

Finally, in this section, we contrast the different techniques in terms of what the teacher does and what the child does during the assessment.

Writing – multiple choice questions

What we mean

MCQs are structured in such a way that the child chooses one, or more than one, answer from a given menu.

Example 1

Who was the British Prime Minister during the Second World War?

    (a) Chamberlain
    (b) Churchill
    (c) Eden
    (d) Attlee

Example 2

If food is frozen, harmful bacteria are killed.
(True or False)

Example 3

Match each of the digital displays to a clock face.

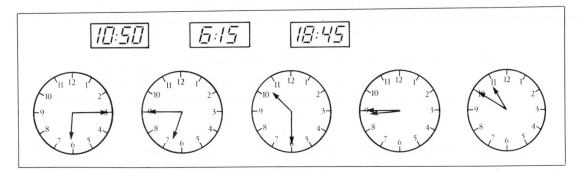

In an MCQ the child discriminates between different choices offered: the questions assess multiple discrimination. In multiple discrimination the child must recall knowledge (as in Example 1) and perhaps go on to demonstrate some measure of comprehension (as in Example 2).

Multiple choice items can be designed to examine the application of concepts and principles, but the questions become very much longer and more complex in structure – and doubts about validity arise because of the facility in language required to interpret them.

Examples of good practice

Here is an example from *Science in Schools*, Report 1, Assessment of Performance Unit, HMSO, 1981, Written Tests, p. 92.

Question page

Look at this picture of people walking through fields in which there are animals.

Read the statements below.
Tick the one statement which you can be most sure is true just by looking at the picture.

☐ The walkers have left the gate open.

☐ Some sheep have strayed in with the cows.

☐ The farmer is going to be angry.

☐ There are some sheep in both fields.

☐ The cows will go into the other field.

Another example is used for assessment on reading in *Language Performance in Schools*, Primary School Report 1, HMSO, 1981, p. 50.

Put a ring round the number of the best answer to each question.

23. *When did men first hunt whales?*

    1.   In the twelfth century.   (24)
    2.   In prehistoric times.   (53)
    3.   In the nineteenth century.   (7)
    4.   In northern waters.   (1)
    5.   In kayaks.   (9)

% correct   53

% omitted   5

> 24. *'New whaling grounds were opened up off Iceland, Newfoundland and the Davis Straits'*
> *What do you think is meant by a 'whaling ground'?*
>
> | | | |
> |---|---|---|
> | 1. | A boatyard that builds whaling ships | (10) |
> | 2. | An island in the sea. | (4) |
> | 3. | An area of sea where whales are caught. | (56) |
> | 4. | A place where whales breed. | (18) |
> | 5. | A factory for processing whales. | (4) |
>
> % correct   56
>
> % omitted   7

Advantages claimed for the technique

The advantages are as follows:

1 there is consistency in marking – it is **reliable**;
2 MCQs can be marked quickly;
3 the content area is sampled better because more questions are asked of the child.

The real advantage of MCQs over other forms of assessment is very often due to the fact that more effort is put in to make them up.

It is frequently claimed by teachers that the major disadvantage in using MCQs is, in fact, the time taken in the construction of good items. While it is true that it can be a time-consuming task, it is possible for the experienced teacher to take short cuts in writing good items by using children's frequently quoted wrong answers to open-ended questions as distractors, and by making the question choices short by formulating a more specific stem.

Writing MCQs is a bit like learning to drive a car. At first you think the task is impossible and that you are a failure. The first two or three questions do have a painful gestation period – but things do improve.

Practical hints

Use the following guide-lines when making up your own MCQs:

1 The instructions must be clear. Answering MCQs is a technique that has to be learned, and young children need careful guidance. They must know what to do, and they must have some practice.
2 Avoid negatives in the statement of the problem in the question.
3 Avoid including clues to the right answer in the stem.
4 When constructing a test, consider the use of items from an item bank of published items.
5 When constructing a test, put the easier items first in order to assist the weaker children.

Most MCQs used in primary classrooms are part of published resources (for example, SRA Reading Kits).

Evaluating the information arising from MCQs

MCQs are not as objective as you might think. There is certainly objectivity in the marking, but subjectivity still arises in the following ways:

• the choice of questions set reflects the individual teacher's subjective view (a different teacher would select different questions and children's scores would be different);
• the choice of standard or grade which will be regarded as satisfactory;
• the varying performance of children.

Do not get too exercised about the problem of guessing. Children seldom guess at random

– they usually make their choice on the basis of partial knowledge.

In a class the range of scores from an MCQ test can often be greater than with other forms of assessment. This reflects the greater sampling of the content area, where a child who knows it well will consistently score high and a child who has poor knowledge will consistently score low. It also reflects the more subjective nature of other forms of assessment where a teacher will use his or her professional judgement to give credit for something which might be there but is not in the scoring system.

The antipathy towards MCQs in the primary school perhaps arises because they were associated with selection examinations for secondary schools. We suggest that they are best used for assessment of acquisition of knowledge, and perhaps also the application of concepts to specific situations.

Writing – sentence completion

What we mean

Many of the everyday questions set by teachers in the classroom involve sentence completion. They are questions which can be answered with a number, a word, a phrase, or, at most, a sentence. For example,

The number which is one less than 2010 is ____.

(Mathematical Development, Primary School Survey 1, Assessment of Performance Unit, HMSO, 1980, p. 38.)

Some of these questions are objective – there is only one correct answer. But answers can be more open-ended. For example,

Write a suitable beginning to this sentence: _____ as it began to snow.

The child has a completely free choice and writes his answer in his own words. Yet, as the examiner merely has to decide whether what is written is grammatically acceptable and reasonably appropriate to the context, there is seldom much doubt about its correctness or incorrectness. Assessment is objective.

Examples of good practice

Consider the question in the figure below from *Primary Mathematics: A Development Through Activity*, by the Scottish Primary Mathematics Group, Stage 4 (Heinemann, 1986, p. 50).

Here the author is assisting the child with a format in order to elicit an answer.

On p. 51 of the same book, there is this example:

The weight of one litre of water is _____.

The author would need to consider what length of line should be drawn: will the child write *1 kg* or *one kilogram*? Not knowing this, some children might be misled by the printed length of line.

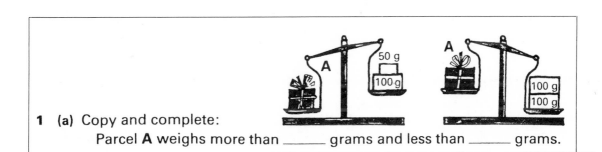

1 (a) Copy and complete:
   Parcel **A** weighs more than _____ grams and less than _____ grams.

Here is another example (from R. Fyfe and E. Mitchell, *Reading Strategies and Their Assessment*, NFER-Nelson, 1985):

Look up each word in **heavy black print** in your dictionary.
Read the meaning and complete the sentence.

1. **Lignin** is the main part of _ _ _ _ _ _ _ _ _ _ _ _

2. A **trug** is a kind of _ _ _ _ _ _ _ _ _ _ _ _

3. If you are **gullible** you are _ _ _ _ _ _ _ _ _ _ _

4. **Orienteering** is a kind of _ _ _ _ _ _ _ _ _ _ _

The following is a completion item – though not sentence completion:

(Assessment of Performance Unit, Mathematical Development, Primary School Survey 2, HMSO, 1981, p. 67.)

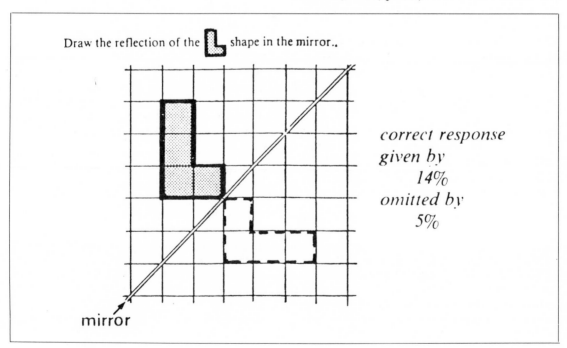

Draw the reflection of the ⌐ shape in the mirror.

correct response given by 14% omitted by 5%

mirror

Advantages claimed for the technique

The advantage claimed for sentence completion items is that the child is given help to express the answer (instead of simply choosing from a menu as in MCQs) and that the questions can be marked as objectively (in effect, reliably) as with MCQs. However, many would claim that answering in order to complete a teacher's sentence means that the child not only has to find the answer but also to make it fit the given sentence, and that this is an important disadvantage.

Consider these three items:

1 The Canadian Shield is an area of ____.
2 Economically the Canadian Shield provides Canada with ____.
3 Human settlement in the Canadian Shield in the past took the form of ____ and future settlement is likely to ____.

Technically the ruled line is called a **formal prompt**. The prompts in item 3 suggest that two words are called for, and in item 1 a longer answer. What is your answer to item 1? Hard rock/lake and forest/low population/no arable land? We could go on. It is not a satisfactory question. And the same applies to items 2 and 3.

Moreover, the formal prompt does not help; if anything, it makes questions more ambiguous.

Practical hints

We do not favour the use of sentence completion items except when it helps the child with the format of the answer. If you do decide to use them, we suggest that:

- the answers should be about important facts – not trivia,
- the prompt should call for one unambiguous answer,
- the prompt (the blank or the line) should be placed near the end of the question,
- items which cover the same content should be grouped together.

Evaluating the information arising from sentence completion

Although the answers are short, they may contain ambiguities and lead to misunderstandings.

Sentence completion can be useful if the results of assessment are to be ignored – if, for example, homework in the form of a test or writing is not always marked. The assumption behind such work is that the child will benefit from completing it. It is an end in itself. More benefit would arise if children were to assess their own work, or each other's. A given form for the answer might help in this instance.

Sentence completion is probably only suitable for the assessment of the acquisition of knowledge.

Writing – answering direct questions

This is the most usual type of question in the primary school. A short answer is expected. Unfortunately, often all the child is given scope for is the answer Yes or No.

The direct question can be presented and responded to both in writing or orally. In both cases the decision has to be made as to how direct you are going to be.

Examples of closed questions

What is the product of 7 times 9?
In what year did the Second World War end?
Who is the present Prime Minister of the United Kingdom?

Normally there are no clues and no prompts, and there is a question mark at the end of the sentence. The answer required is short. Because of their closed nature such questions can be used to assess the acquisition of knowledge by the child demonstrating recall or comprehension.

Examples of more open questions

What two numbers multiplied together give the answer 24?

Describe someone who might live on the island.

The more open the question becomes, the more likely it is to assess more than the acquisition of knowledge. The disadvantage is that it is not always clear to the learner just what is expected of him or her.

Advantages claimed for the technique

The main advantage claimed for direct questions is that they are unprompted.

Practical hints

Perhaps the greatest dangers in developing a direct question for use in assessment are the following, and these can be avoided:

1 An open-ended question would be quite appropriate for a piece of writing but is much less appropriate for a very short answer. A range of short answers arising from an open-ended question can be very difficult to assess. So, normally, direct questions should be closed questions leading to a predictable and easily assessable answer.
2 Although direct questions are commonly used and are perhaps the easiest to construct, they can focus on the trivial and the irrelevant, simply because it is easy to identify a clear point on which to pose a question. For example, in history, it is very easy to focus on dates and names.
3 Avoid constructing questions where the child can answer Yes or No.

The way to approach the development of direct questions for assessment purposes is first to decide on the answer you want and then to construct a question to give you that answer.

Evaluating the information arising from direct questions

Direct questions can be used to assess the acquisition of knowledge and the ability to apply concepts and principles. They are much less appropriate for assessing a child's ability to communicate, to solve problems, or to determine a child's attitude (assessment of attitude by direct question is the same as a questionnaire, and we have already stated how invalid these can be).

If you find a test consisting of direct questions requiring short answers, the chances are that it focuses on assessing the acquisition of knowledge and comprehension, and the results should be interpreted accordingly.

Extended writing

What we mean

Asking the child to write allows scope for children to organise knowledge and concepts with which to tackle new situations. The open-endedness allows for originality and imagination, so there is little point in using this as a test of recall of factual information. Writing can be used to assess the application of concepts to specific situations (although this is often best done by providing the child with the practical situations), problem solving and attitudes. Two criteria would form the basis of whether or not to use writing. These are:

1 If the answers are to be restricted in advance, then writing should not be used.
2 If the content to be sampled is wide, then using MCQs or short-answer questions will enable much more ground to be covered in a short time. However, if sam-

pling across a wide range of the curriculum is less important than assessing fewer ideas in depth, then writing is more appropriate.

The teacher should have a clear idea of the answer expected and then design a title which is tight enough to give this. General titles which give no guidance to the child will be difficult to assess.

Example 1

> Read the account of the sighting of a strange object in the sky. Then read the 'Advice for UFO Spotters'.
>
> Imagine that you are the person in the story and that you wish to report your experience to the Ministry of Defence. *Following the advice given*, write a report of what you saw.

Example 2

> Imagine this scene:
>> A tall ragged man is trudging up a steep muddy lane. A little girl and an old woman are hurrying after him. It is pouring with rain. The man looks grim and determined. The little girl and old woman look frightened.
>
> Write a story about this scene. If you like, your story could answer some of these questions.
>> Who are these people?
>> Where are they going?
>> Where have they come from?
>> Is something going to happen, or has it already happened?

Examples of good practice

Below are two examples taken from Language Performance in Schools, Primary School Report 1, HMSO, 1981, pp. 95 and 99.

Advantages claimed for the technique

The main advantage claimed for writing as an instrument of assessment is that the work of the child is unprompted, that it allows free association. For this reason the focus of assessment should be on communication and on attitudes.

If the focus is on the application of concepts or principles to specific situations, it is important that the situation is specified to the child. This means that the title of the essay has to be long (as in the examples given in the previous section). Given this proviso, writing can be used for the assessment of the application of concepts and principles.

If the focus is on problem solving, a piece of writing can be an appropriate way of communicating the results of the problem-solving activity. For example,

> Make up a game for three players which is about spelling words.
> Write the rules of your game.

If the problem solving is built round the

writing activity, then a modified essay question (**MEQ**) is appropriate.

Practical hints

If you want the child to follow through a certain process, suggest sub-headings in your task (see the second example given, on page 27). If it is imagination you are after, give the base line from which imagination is to take off.

Decide in advance if you are going to mark analytically using a checklist of important points, or impressionistically. The answers to this decision depend on what you are trying to test:

- if you are checking concepts and principles (recall, comprehension and application), then mark analytically;
- if you are assessing problem solving or attitudes, then mark holistically.

Think how you are going to give the child feedback on the writing, or how it is to be marked, when making up the question. This will eliminate weaknesses in the title and improve reliability in giving feedback or marking.

Allow sufficient time for the children with learning difficulties. If a **power test** is intended, questions with short answers should be used.

Evaluating the information arising from extended writing

Most writing is used as formative assessment by teachers. Writing alerts the teacher to strengths and weaknesses and, better still, provides information as to what are the children's difficulties. However, the full diagnosis of such difficulties usually requires something more than writing alone.

If the main purpose is formative, it is essential that there is teaching and discussion about writing to help children to develop fluency, creativity and techniques, to correct faults and extend strengths. Emphasise to the child what he or she would have to do to improve their standard of writing.

It is very difficult to use writing in **criterion-test** situations – the questions have to be clear and explicit.

Assessment of writing is **norm-referenced**: ideally, the task is set in such a way that the able children can be stretched but the less able can still do something. This means that if the results are to be recorded, and passed on to someone else, it is important to make clear the group within which the comparison is being made.

Assessment activities

In the primary school, children often work in groups to carry out a task. It is often necessary for the teacher to find out the individual's progress in such group work.

The setting of a practical task for the individual can give feedback on the child's ability to

- select equipment,
- use it effectively,
- provide an end product, and/or
- record an oral response.

The emphasis can be on monitoring the process which the child uses or on the end product. Ideally, the teacher should observe what the individual does. However, if several children are carrying out such activities, observation of each child is limited, although this is usually enough when considered alongside a short written answer and/or an end product.

The task should be written on a card and all the materials required provided. Most children should be able to carry out the task in three or four minutes.

Examples of good practice

The examples below are taken from A. Duncan and L. Mitchell, *Assessment Activities in Mathematics* (Jordanhill College of Education, 1986.)

VOLUME LEVEL 3

> Use the cubes.
> Make a shape with a volume of **18 cubic centimetres**.

NUMBER LEVEL 4

> Read this problem and find the answer.
> Mrs Jones makes 84 puppets a week.
> Mrs Wills makes 400 puppets a month.
> Who makes **more** puppets in a year? **How many** more?
> Tell the tape recorder your name and what you did to find the answer.

The following example is from *Science in Schools, Age 11*, Report No. 1, HMSO, 1981, Practical Tests, p. 132.

Sugar lumps

Find out if the sugar lumps dissolve more quickly than ordinary loose sugar.
Try this first *stirring* the water.
Then see which dissolves more quickly when you do not stir the water.

(a) Write down here any results and working as you go along:

(b) Write down here what you found:
When the water was stirred the one which dissolved more quickly was ....

When the water was not stirred the one which dissolved more quickly was ....

These final examples are from the project funded by the Scottish Education Department, 'Practical Assessment of Environmental Studies in the Primary School' (1981–4). From 'The Weather', for P3 children:

```
Look out at the sky.

Choose a card to match what you see.

Today is  [            ]
```

From 'How Things Change', for P6/7 children:

```
Here is some food.  Each item has been preserved.

Use the tape recorder.  Say your name.

Say what method you think has been used to preserve
each item.

Explain how this has changed the food.
```

Advantages claimed for the technique

Some teachers would claim this technique to be 'a window on the child's understanding'. From research findings, there seems little doubt that the teacher can gain a great deal of feedback about the child's understanding of concepts. Most teachers who have used this technique are amazed at the assumptions they have made about children's understanding of 'ordinary' concepts and their ability to select and use equipment. One P6 teacher, who had just completed a project on transport in Grampian, carried out some practical assessment activities and discovered two children who coloured a map to make Grampian Region an island! A P4 teacher, assessing mathematics practically, realised that one child was having difficulty in interpreting the question. On enquiry, the teacher discovered he was trying to decide which of two centicube shapes was the 'louder' for a question which asked for the shape with greater 'volume'!

Practical hints

The assessment activities should be devised in order to determine if the child can carry out one or, at most two, specific objectives. A bank of activities should be shared by teachers so that the effort used in making these up, and collating the required materials, is used to maximum advantage.

The teacher can put out one or two practical assessment activities at the side of the room and ask each child in a group to go, in turn, to carry these out. Occasionally the teacher may want the activity to be out of view of the other children. The materials and the instruction card are then placed, for example, behind a bookshelf or just outside the door.

Every child in the class could have the opportunity to attempt an activity or , alternatively, the teacher could confine the activity to a selected few.

Another method of using assessment activities is to set out two more than the number of children in the group to be assessed. For example, the teacher sets out ten assessment activities and selects eight children to attempt them. A child is allocated to one of the activities and told that when this is completed he is to go to any other which is free until all the activities have been tackled. Usually, the children are told they have a specific time for this – for example, for ten activities a maximum time is likely to be about 50 minutes.

Evaluating the information arising from assessment activities

The teacher can leave the children to carry out the activities without supervision. This means that she assesses the activity by looking at either an end product or a short written answer. She may have to listen to a taped oral response.

The teacher will find it worthwhile working with a group near the activities so that any unexpected behaviour by a child can be noted and discussed later. If several activities are used for a group, the teacher should set work for the other children in the class and monitor the assessment activities by the technique called structured observation and listening, which is described in detail in the next section.

It is interesting to quote the APU *Science in Schools* Survey Report (HMSO, 1981): 'In particular high priority was given to the inclusion of practical tests' and 'many aspects of children's work that we have tried to test [through practical activities] have never been tested before in a comprehensive manner at any level.'

Structured observation and listening

Teachers have always looked at and listened to the children in their class. However, the value of using these techniques as tools of assessment is much more recent. The child is given a task, and is observed carrying out the task. He or she is assessed on the process used by the child – what he or she does. Both the **validity** and **reliability** of the assessment can be improved through the use of a checklist to structure the observations.

The teacher can consider structured listening as asking a child prepared questions about his or her own view of what is being learned, what progress is being made and what difficulties are being experienced.

Examples of good practice

In the series *We've Done It* by A. Duncan, K. Dundas, N. Henderson and A. Morris (Ginn, 1987), checklists are used to monitor the individual child's progress as children in a small group work together to solve problems. Here is part of the checklist given in the Red Starter Pack in this series. It is intended for a teacher observing two or three 6- to 8-year-old children engaged in solving the following problem:

Build one large cube using the 8 little cubes.

Each face must show four different colours of squares.

Materials   8 cubes identical in size and of these colours 2 red, 2 blue, 2 yellow and 2 green.

Here is the suggested checklist:

Children's Names

The child:				
1 does not rush into action.				
2 realises what the instructions mean.				
3 participates in deciding what to do.				
4 is aware of all the materials provided.				
5 suggests how some of the materials can be used.				
6 talks with the others.				
7 listens to what the others are saying.				
8 shares the materials.				
9 shares the task.				
10 wants to make the solution as good as possible.				
11 shows imagination and originality.				
12 works neatly.				

Advantages claimed for the technique

The main advantage of the technique is that it enables the teacher to assess the process or processes used by the child in completing the task. If the processes are only partially understood, this will suggest guidelines for remedial measures.

Because the technique is somewhat time-consuming as far as the teacher is concerned, we suggest that it only be used for the assessment of problem solving and the application of concepts and principles to specific situations. Data on communication and attitudes can also arise from these situations.

Practical hints

1 Do not try to observe more than three children at any one observation session.
2 Listen as you observe.
3 If you devise your own checklist, link it to the learning objectives you wish to assess.
4 The checklist should be a list of 'actions' you expect the child to take.
5 Value the children's own assessment of their learning.
6 Devise questions which help the children to tell about what they find difficult, what they find too easy, and their concerns about their learning. Listen to what they have to say.

Evaluating the information arising from structured observation and listening

With structured observation and listening the focus for assessment is on process. Sometimes the process can be inferred from the end product, so no observation of the process is required: the children can be left to get on with it. This is what happens with many practical activities. Other activities do require observation. Observation is structured through the use of a checklist.

The child should be assessed by observation and listening across a range of curricular activities.

Informal assessment

What we mean

Much informal assessment takes place in the classroom. The advantage lies in observing children in natural situations rather than formal situations imposed by the assessment procedures.

We believe that there is a strong case for developing this type of assessment by trying to maintain the spontaneity of the situation yet becoming more alert to the kinds of information which can arise from this type of activity. This can be achieved by having a programme of informal observation of children, and noting the results, to assist the building of a profile of the individual child. This reflects the changing philosophy in the primary school with increasing emphasis on the individual child, his needs, his interests, his progress and his problems.

Examples of good practice

Informal observation can give you feedback on your teaching and organisation. For example,

you could monitor a few children for the first three minutes in each school hour for a day, and obtain data about how much children in your classroom are engaged in meaningful learning.

To find out, for instance, a child's stage of awareness in litter consciousness, give the children a task which involves cutting paper. You may perhaps tell them to cut out three symmetrical quadrilaterals. As they work – and unknown to the children – you will be monitoring individual attitudes to the scrap paper produced.

Advantages claimed for the technique

The main advantage of this technique is that it can yield information on

- the more advanced stages in the development of curriculum attitudes,
- the social behaviour of the child, and
- the health of the child.

Practical hints

The most important and perhaps the most difficult aspect of informal assessment is for the teacher constantly to be alert to its possibilities. How often have we recognised that signs have been around for a while and that we have been slow to recognise them? We propose a more systematic programme of informal observation of the children, perhaps focusing on two children for a week.

For example, in the classroom the teacher might assess whether or not the child

1 gives his or her full attention to the task,
2 sustains attention throughout the task,
3 is particularly restless,
4 tries to catch the teacher's attention,
5 is keen to answer questions,
6 reacts, with concern, to his or her final score of correct answers,

7 wants to know why an answer is wrong, or
8 appreciates the help the teacher offers about wrong answers.

On another occasion, the teacher might decide to use the time when the children are getting ready and moving to the hall for physical education. Again, some observations can be made about whether the individual child

1 organises clothing and shoes as he or she collects them and changes into them,
2 offers help to others with knots in shoe-laces or other problems,
3 gives full attention to getting ready,
4 socialises as he or she gets ready,
5 takes the initiative in holding doors open, turning out lights . . . and so on.

These points reveal aspects of the daily routine which can provide an informal assessment setting. No formal recording should be necessary, but notes could be useful when linking the information gathered to other assessments and when writing child profiles.

Evaluating the information arising from informal assessment

Informal assessment without some underlying plan very often tells you more about the assessor than the assessed. The reason for this is that we suffer from selective observation and selective memory. It is in order to counter this bias that we propose an observational schedule.

However, checklists are not recommended. This is a much more open-ended situation, with the emphasis on the teacher's professional judgement as to information which will usefully complement the data gathered in the more formal situations – all helping to build a fuller profile of the individual child.

Published tests and inventories

What we mean

The difficulties in constructing tests are apparent. It would certainly save the teacher time if tests could be bought ready made – and indeed some can be bought.

It is difficult to find tests which match the curriculum needs, given the curriculum diversity we have in the United Kingdom – this is quite a different matter in, for example, Scandinavian countries which have a highly centralised curriculum. For this reason published tests are to be approached with caution and, equally, the results from these tests evaluated with caution.

Examples of good practice

Published tests are available for

reading	psychological
language	factors
mathematics	intelligence
composite	personality
attainments	counselling

The book, P. Levy and H. Goldstein, *Tests in Education: A Book of Critical Reviews* (London: Academic Press, 1984), contains a list of 140 tests which are available in United Kingdom, where each can be obtained, and a critical review of each. Every primary school should have access to this book.

Some of the published tests are, in effect, questionnaires which are aimed at the assessment of attitudes.

Advantages claimed for the technique

Most published tests assume achievements which are general attributes independent of the immediate context – for example, reading, mathematics, verbal reasoning or even personality. But professional judgement tells us that such assumptions are not valid.

Practical hints

You should be interested in the information that comes with the test, what the test purports to measure, the population on which the test has been piloted and the curricular assumption that lies behind the test. Published tests should

- state clearly what they purport to assess,
- be constructed on the basis of trials,
- be standardised (this usually means that they are norm-referenced),
- include standard procedures for administration,
- give guide-lines for the interpretation of the data.

Evaluating the information arising from published tests and inventories

Remember that the test result is only one part of the assessment. Because it is apparently an 'objective test', this suggests that it is an assessment superior to subjective professional judgement – but this is certainly not true. Do not use the results of a published test unsupported by other evidence.

Perhaps the main reason for using published tests is that through norm-referencing teachers can see how the children in their class, or a particular group or an individual compares with a wider group in which the test has been standardised. Such tests can also give some idea of progress, although, as has been emphasised, the results must be treated with caution.

Comparison of techniques

Technique	What the teacher does	What the child does
MCQs	Presents the question in written form. Corrects as right or wrong. Gives a score.	Indicates choices.
Sentence completion	Presents the question in written form or is aware when it occurs in textbook material. Corrects as right or wrong. Sometimes gives a score.	Writes one- or two-word answers.
Answering direct questions	Presents the questions either orally, in writing or from textbook material. In the oral situation, the teacher can encourage improved answers and find out reasons for incorrect answers or misunderstandings. In the written situation, marks as correct or incorrect. Sometimes gives a score.	Responds orally or in writing, usually with short answers.

Technique	What the teacher does	What the child does
Extended writing	Presents the question in written form or in textbook materials. Makes corrections of spelling, grammar and punctuation. Can offer help with overall structure, sentence construction, expressing ideas, wider vocabulary.	Responds in writing – usually at length.
Assessment activities	Usually presents the question in written form on a card. Observation is unstructured. Finds out a child's manipulative ability, strategies for finding a solution, understanding of concepts, and oral fluency if taping is involved.	Given specific tasks, responds by taking action, e.g. measuring building, making, taping, etc. Sometimes there are also one or two short written answers.
Structured observation and listening	Looks and/or listens to a structure, records on a checklist initially and then makes an entry in the child's profile.	Carries on with the set task which involves action and/or communication. Is aware of being assessed.
Informal assessment	Carries on with the usual daily procedures but selects one or two aspects of behaviour to note during a specific time. These can be within or outside the classroom. Uses the observations noted for entries in the child's profile.	Carries on with the daily routine unaware that assessment is taking place.

In previous chapters we have compared assessment and evaluation, suggested a classification for assessing the curriculum, and detailed the techniques for the teacher to use. These aspects become much clearer when they are related to classroom practice. In this chapter we provide the teacher with situations which require assessment decisions. We show how a teacher might make these decisions and carry out the assessment.

For each example, we will suggest:

1 the *classification* of the assessment,
2 any *assessment principles* involved,
3 the *technique* to be used,
4 the *form* the assessment task(s) might take,
5 *examples* of a few children's responses to the suggested assessment tasks, and/or
6 the *evaluation* of these made by the teacher.

The main emphasis is on showing you how to tackle your own assessment needs. The assessment situations and the specific solutions are only examples. If previously you have only used written assessment, the examples should help you to combine written assessment with other techniques. This could be your introduction to using other forms of assessment.

Example 1

The teacher wants to check subtraction of tens and units with her class. She wants to find out if the children can do examples like the following:

$$\begin{array}{r} 42 \\ -\ 25 \\ \hline \end{array} \quad\text{and}\quad \begin{array}{r} 53 \\ -\ 36 \\ \hline \end{array}$$

Classification of assessment

The focus of assessment is on the *acquisition of knowledge*. At this stage the teacher is focusing her interest on whether or not the children have comprehended the method of 'decomposing' a ten, rather than looking at the need to 'decompose' or the ability to apply the principle of subtraction to a new situation.

Principles of assessment

The assessment should be *criterion referenced*.

Technique of assessment

The technique could be *answering questions*.

Form of the assessment

The form could be *written examples*.

The written task will consist of five examples to sample the field. This is sufficient to gather information. The criterion of mastery should be at least four out of five correct.

Each child should have as long as he or she needs for the task.

The assessment task

Name		Age	Date	
42 − 25	53 − 36	60 − 12	74 − 58	96 − 47

All the examples involve decomposition because this is what the teacher wishes to focus on. The example with the zero has deliberately been put in the middle. The teacher realises that this is likely to cause difficulty and she wishes to find out how such a difficulty affects the examples which follow.

Some children's responses

These children were at the beginning of their fourth year of schooling. After two weeks, their new teacher wished to assess their knowledge of subtraction. She had made an informal judgement and placed the children in the categories 'Seem able to carry out the decomposition process' and 'Seem unable to carry out the decomposition process'. Now she wanted some evidence before proceeding further.

Here are the responses of three children thought to be competent, followed by three whose competence was in doubt.

Name Scott C **Age** 7 **Date** Friday

$$\begin{array}{r} 42 \\ -25 \\ \hline \end{array}\ 23 \quad \begin{array}{r} 53 \\ -36 \\ \hline \end{array}\ 23 \quad \begin{array}{r} 60 \\ -12 \\ \hline \end{array}\ 52 \quad \begin{array}{r} 74 \\ -58 \\ \hline \end{array}\ 24 \quad \begin{array}{r} 96 \\ -47 \\ \hline \end{array}\ 51$$

Name Aziz **Age** 8 **Date** 12 th

$$17 \quad 17 \quad 68 \quad 16 \quad 49$$

Name Craig **Age** 8 **Date** Friday

$$\begin{array}{r} 42 \\ -25 \\ \hline \end{array}\ 23 \quad \begin{array}{r} 53 \\ -36 \\ \hline \end{array}\ 23 \quad \begin{array}{r} 60 \\ -12 \\ \hline \end{array}\ 5 \quad \begin{array}{r} 74 \\ -58 \\ \hline \end{array}\ 23 \quad \begin{array}{r} 96 \\ -47 \\ \hline \end{array}\ 50$$

The teacher's evaluation

Here are the teacher's comments on each of these children. The teacher's method of record keeping is to attach these comments to the tests. Each is kept in the child's folder of 'special' work.

Steven

I thought Steven would be competent. I notice he has the confidence not to use crutch figures. In the last calculation, this has led him to getting the wrong answer as he seems to have forgotten he is taking 4 tens from 8 tens. I spoke to him about this calculation. He realised that he had made a mistake and has undertaken to check his work watching out for this type of error.

Jamie

Jamie seems to be able to carry out subtractions quickly and accurately with confidence.

Sharon

I realise that Sharon is not as competent as I had thought. She begins confidently and has the first two examples correct. The example with 0 has upset her and shaken her confidence. She has taken the 'easy way' out of the difficulty by subtracting the smaller number from the larger. Unfortunately, she adopts this policy for the units in the next calculation. In the last one it is difficult to know how Sharon got her units answer. She can't explain it herself.

Scott C

My worries about Scott are justified. In each example he has taken the top smaller unit digit from the lower larger one, and the lower smaller tens digit from the larger upper digit. He doesn't seem to realise the calculation he is setting out to do, or if he does, the need for decomposing a ten. He certainly does seem to know his basic subtraction facts with numbers 0 to 9.

40

Aziz

This is much better than I had expected. Aziz has managed all but one of the subtractions successfully. He realised as soon as I asked him to look at the calculation again that he had added 1 to the tens instead of taking it away. Does this indicate that it is a mechanical process which he doesn't really understand? I'll have to check further.

Craig

Craig has many difficulties. He attempts to take the smaller number from the larger, regardless of position. He doesn't manage to do this correctly. He was very worried by the zero and after a great deal of thought was unable to complete this part of the calculation.

Overall comment

A comment like this, but referring to all the children, is written in the teacher's class record of work:

Steven, Jamie and Aziz have shown an acceptable knowledge of the recorded process of subtraction by having 4 or 5 of the calculations correct. Sharon needs more practice in subtraction to be secure about the process and requires help with examples containing zero. Scott C needs to begin decomposition again. Craig does not appear ready for computation with tens and units. I shall want to carry out further assessment before planning his programme of work.

Example 2

On the basis of the test developed for the previous situation, the teacher discovered that three children cannot carry out subtraction of tens and units, involving decomposition, competently. Two children did not do any of the examples correctly, and a third had only two correct. All the rest of the class had four or five correct.

The teacher wishes to find out more about these children's difficulties.

Classification of assessment

The focus of assessment is on

1 the *acquisition of knowledge* of
   (a) subtraction facts, e.g. $12 - 7$,
   (b) place value, e.g. 42 is 4 tens and 2 units;
2 the *ability to apply these principles* to the subtraction process.

Principles of assessment

Each child is assessed individually and *diagnostically*.

Technique of assessment

The technique could be *assessment activities*.

Form of assessment

Each activity, with an instruction card and all the materials required, should be laid out for the children to attempt individually.

One activity could be a matching game where the child matches a card with a subtraction fact to a card with the answer.

Another activity could involve representing a number by ten-rods and unit-cubes.

A third activity could require the child to subtract a number of units by decomposing a ten rod and then recording this action as a calculation.

A fourth activity could involve the child in recording orally on tape the steps taken in a subtraction calculation.

The organisation involved for the children to attempt activities like these varies. The simplest method is to put out the first activity (followed by the second, and so on) at the side of the room and allow each child in turn to tackle it. This minimises preparation and allows the teacher to be on hand to explain instructions, if necessary, and to look at answers immediately after the child has completed the activity. The teacher will then be in a position to decide immediately if a child should be asked to attempt any further activities. This organisation places no constraints on the children regarding time or the necessity to undertake one activity immediately after another.

The assessment tasks

Activity A

Instruction card
Match each take-away sum with its answer. Find the take-away sum with the wrong answer.

Materials
The following calculations and answers, each written on a separate card.

10 − 7	3	15 − 9	6
12 − 8	4	14 − 9	5
13 − 6*	8		

* This is the calculation for which there is no correct answer as only 8 is left unpaired.

Activity B

Instruction card
Show 42 with the tens and units.

Put the tens and units in an envelope. Write your name on the envelope.

Materials
A box of ten-rods and unit-cubes, envelopes.
A box labelled 'Put your envelopes here'.

Activity C

Instruction card
Take the tens and units out of an envelope.
Write the number.
Take 8 away.
Write the take away sum you have done.

Materials
Envelopes which contain three ten-rods and five unit-cubes and a piece of paper for each child, a box of ten rods and unit-cubes, a box to 'post' the 'answer' paper.

Activity D

Instruction card
Do this take-away sum.

$$\begin{array}{r} 51 \\ -\,27 \\ \hline \end{array}$$

Use tens and units. Say each step as you do it on tape.

Materials
A box of ten-rods and unit-cubes. A tape recorder with a blank tape (record, play and pause buttons should be depressed). The children should know how to use the tape recorder or another child should be there to operate it for all the children.

The teacher's evaluation of the children's responses

Opposite are the teacher's comments on what the children did.

Activity A – teen subtraction facts

Sharon and Scott C completed the matching activity without difficulty. Sharon took quite a long time as she checked the cards she had matched. Craig was not successful. He seemed to know what he had to do, possibly from seeing the others pair the cards, but he did not match the correct answers.

Activity B – place value

Craig again had difficulty. He laid out two ten-rods and four unit-cubes. The others did the activity correctly. They all enjoyed writing their name on an envelope. It seems sensible to take the understanding of the written two-digit numbers as a beginning for a programme of work for Craig and not to ask him to attempt any more of the assessment activities.

Activity C – recording a subtraction

Sharon and Scott C both found this difficult. I think it was because the first number is not visible after the eight units are physically removed. I must give the children more help to organise how they use the tens and units.

Activity D – talking through a subtraction

Sharon and Scott C were hesitant about saying what they were doing. I must give both more practice in using the tape recorder, preferably in an informal situation where they can record anything they like and then listen to their own voices. I must also make sure I ask them to talk about numbers and what they do in calculations whenever I can.

I will have to rethink the way the children use the structured number pieces. They have been taught to put out both numbers in the subtraction to give the same layout as the written calculation. This is what I have been doing too, but I can see that this is leading to confusion for these children. Because both unit numbers are represented, it is possible for them to subtract the one unit from the seven units. This is what Scott C tried to do. Sharon did not fall into this trap, but was worried about what to do with the two tens and seven units which she had set out. I think both children will benefit from a new approach. I shall show them how to put out pieces for the larger number only. The smaller number can be shown with numeral cards to remind them what to take away. They can place the 'taken-away' pieces on the numeral cards and place the pieces left in the answer section.

tens	units
	□
2	7

Sharon miscounted the ten units when she made the exchange in the assessment activity. The children should be encouraged to *match* the units to the ten rather than count them.

I decided to try out this last activity with Steven, Aziz and Jamie. These are children who have shown competence in written work. I wanted to check on their understanding of the process as a sample of the rest of the class.

All of these children put out both numbers as taught but ignored the twenty-seven. All began with the tens. From the five tens they took away two tens, then looked at a third ten and either put it in the box and took out three units, or counted up the seven units and realised three remain. In other words, they knew what subtraction was about and had developed their own mixture of decomposition and complementary addition. This is excellent. It shows what other children might be taught when they become confident in a written method. Some children may not reach this stage for some time, if at all. For the children using the 'mental method', the crutch figures may cause some confusion. If they can manage successfully without them, I shall accept this.

Overall comment

The assessment has revealed many aspects of using material and carrying out the subtraction process that I hadn't thought about before. I intend to raise how to teach subtraction with the head and assistant head and find out if it is possible to have a staff discussion about it. We could use the children's work as a focus for discussion about how to set out the pieces, what language to use, how to record, and how to develop the children's method from written to mental.

Example 3

The local Rotary Club, prompted by the school's Parent Teacher Association, has offered to fund attendance at a computer course in London for the most mathematically talented child in the school.

The school has expressed reservations about singling out one child in this way, but has decided that the opportunity for that one child warrants that the school accept the offer.

Three teachers are asked to meet with the headteacher to decide how the school will select the child.

Classification of assessment

The group decide the focus of assessment would be on *problem solving*.

The children will be assessed on their ability to select from their concepts and principles of mathematics and to apply these to questions and practical situations which have not been met before.

Principles of assessment

The assessment is *norm referenced*.

The teachers would have welcomed a criterion-referenced situation where they could send all the children who met a specific standard on the course.

Technique of assessment

A number of techniques would be used here:

- *answering questions*;
- *assessment activities*;
- *structured observation*.

Form of the assessment

The group believed that the assessment material should be suitable for children in a range of classes. However, London is a long way from home for the younger children and so it was decided to limit the assessment to children in P6 and P7.

The group decided the following:

- 'Answering questions' would be implemented by a written **power test**. The use of a published test was considered, but one of the teachers offered to make up a suitable test.
- The assessment activities would involve the child in using a calculator, using a computer program and giving an opinion on tape. Another teacher offered to devise these.
- Structured observation would mean devising a problem for the children to solve in small groups and compiling a checklist for an observer to note each child's problem-

solving behaviour – e.g. generating ideas, modifying an idea. A third teacher offered to plan this.

The power test would be attempted by all children in the selected classes who wished to be considered as a potential applicant for the computer course. For practical purposes, only a selection of these would be assessed by the other two techniques.

The assessment tasks

The power test

The following written power test has a time limit of 20 minutes. The test has a mathematical context but language is emphasised. Remember, it was decided that it was the ability to solve problems – to select concepts and principles as well as to apply them – which is to be assessed through all the techniques.

> *Name*   *Class*   *Age*

1   Fiona is twice as old as you are. What is her age?
2(a) Is six times nineteen about 80, 100, or 120?
  (b) How did you choose that answer?
3   Write *one number* which is
>>   greater than fifty,
>>   less than one hundred,
>>   divides exactly by three, and
>>   is even.
4   What is the largest number you can make with the digits 4, 7, 1 and 3?
5   Some children were asked to half this rectangle. Ben said that each of his halves were squares. Roy said that each of his halves were triangles.

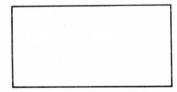

What do you think?

6   Helen made this shape with cubes. How many did she use?

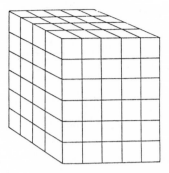

7(a) How long does it take the minute hand of a clock to move from 12 to 6?
  (b) What does the hour hand do as the minute hand moves from 12 to 6?

8(a) Which do you like better, the digital display or the clock face with two hands to tell you the time?
  (b) Give three reasons why this is better.
9   What does the word 'early' mean?
10 Here are some numbers which all tell us about the packet of biscuits on the table. What do you think each of these numbers is telling us about?

(a) 39 p   (b) 200 g
(c) 29 November   (d) 7 cm
(e) 833 cm^3 (f) 1526
(g) 30.

11 About what weight would you think these would be:
(a) a week-old baby (b) a fat man
(c) a car.

12 Think of a mathematics word that begins with 'a', one that begins with 'b' and one with 'c'.

13(a) Find two more numbers for this pattern:
2, 5, 11, 23, ——, ——.
(b) How did you find these numbers?

14(a) Put a number in each box so that the answer is correct:

(b) Put a different number in each box to get the same answer:

$$\square \div \square - \square = 6$$

Materials
The children were given the questions spaced out so that the answers could be filled in on the sheets. An empty biscuit packet was placed at each group table for the children to handle when answering question 10.

Assessment activities

Each activity was set out with an instruction card and all the required materials. The children can be directed to attempt them in turn.

Activity A

Instruction card
Find the first number after 100 which divides exactly by 13.

Materials
A calculator.

Activity B

Instruction card
Look at these shapes.
They all belong to the family of prisms.
Write what you think a prism is.
Now, look in the bag.
The shape in the bag is a prism too.
Now, write a better description of a prism if you want to.

Materials
A cuboid, a triangular prism and a hexagonal prism, and a bag with a cylinder hidden in it.

Activity C

No Instruction card is required as the computer program gives the child instructions.

Materials
BBC Computer and the SPMG Program – *Draw a Shape* (Heinemann, 1986).

Structured observation and listening

The selected children were put into groups of three or four. Each group was given this problem, written on an instruction card, to solve.

Michael finds it difficult to remember all the multiplication facts.
Make an easy-to-carry, easy-to-look-at, card for him to use.

Materials
One sheet of card, one pencil or pen, scissors.

As the group discussed what to do and make their 'card', the observation sheet shown opposite was marked for each child. A tick was marked when a behaviour was noted. Sometimes short comments were added.

The child			
1 offers ideas towards a solution			
2 has ideas which are original and/or creative			
3 listens to what others say			
4 can build on what others say			
5 shares the task			

The teacher's evaluation of the children's responses

Power Test

Comment on individual questions:

1   It was expected that all the children would get this question correct. The child's own age was written just above the question. Some children, however, gave the wrong answer. They had difficulty in interpreting the word 'twice'.

2(a)   About half of the children assessed had difficulty with this question. Those who found it difficult misinterpreted 'six times nineteen' or guessed rather than estimated. Most of those who were correct carried out the multiplication 6×19, not 6×20.

(b)   One girl who chose 80 for the first part of the question justified this choice by writing 'It sounds too silly to be 100 or more if it is 6×19'. A boy who estimated 120 wrote 'it is the highest'. Tracy wrote 'Because 114 is nearer to 120 than 100 and 80'.

3   This question proved very difficult. Was it because there were too many conditions? Only two children gave an acceptable answer – Tracy with 54 and Donna with 60. Many either forgot to make the number even or did not seem to understand what an even number is in this number range.

4   Most had this question correct.

5   Most of the children thought Ben was correct. A few thought Roy was correct. None thought that both could be correct. They were not used to a mathematics question having two correct answers, but possibly the question led them to make one choice.

6   No one had the correct number of cubes. This should have been an easy question. The children did not seem to have had enough experience in building shapes like this – or was it the drawing? The most popular answer was 74 because the children counted the squares they could see, forgetting, or not realising, they were supposed to be counting cubes.

7(a)   The children found this difficult. They probably had not thought previously about the movement of the hands of the clock in this way. About a third of them, however, were correct with '30 minutes'.

(b)   There were only two reasonable

answers here: Tracy wrote that the hour hand 'moves one place on', and Lyne had 'moves on to the next hour'. No one gave the answer: 'It moves half-way to the next number.' Some thought 'it doesn't move', and others wrote, 'the hour hand goes to 12 again'. Rod wrote 'tics'.

8(a) This answer was the expression of an opinion. It was interesting to note that half the children preferred each type.

(b) Here three sensible reasons were required to support the choice of the digital or the traditional clock face. Sometimes the same reason was expressed in two ways; for example, 'it doesn't stop' and 'I don't have to wind it up'. David preferred the digital watch and wrote: '1 Because it shows you the numbers better. 2 It lights up in the dark. 3 And it shows you the seconds going up all the time.'

9 The answers here fell into two categories. One way is to interpret 'early' specifically meaning 'in the morning'; for example, Yvonne wrote, 'it means about 7.00 or it is still dark'. The other way is to generalise the meaning; for example, as Lyne explains, 'early means you are there before the time you were to be there'. Robert wrote 'not late', and Linda expressed it as 'you are quicker than you thought'.

10 This question was a good discriminator among the children.

All knew 39 p was the price.

Only a few could not express 200 g as the weight: Rod wrote 'grams', Yvonne wrote 'it has 200 g', and Angela wrote 'chocolate'.

November 29th was interpreted as 'the date for flinging out' by David and 'date by which it should be sold' by Tracy. Most of the others gave explanations like 'best before' repeating the words on the packet, or 'the date' or did not answer.

7cm was referred to as 'how high', 'the length', 'the width' and 'across the packet' allowing range of language.

No one picked up the clue of cm^3 as a unit of volume.

1526 was found by the children printed on the packet and taken to be 'the number which means how many packets have been sold' by David, 'the number of the packet' by Tracy and Yvonne. The last two answers explained the reference number very well indeed.

David and Linda were the only two to think of 30 being the number of biscuits the packet contained.

11 This question showed clearly whether the children could refer to units of weight meaningfully. David's baby was a hefty 18 lb 6 oz while Tracy's was a lightweight at 7 lb 2 oz, Lyne's 13 lb 6 oz and Yvonne's 8 lb.

Weights for the fat man were '18 stone 15 kg', '12 stone 7', '11 stone 6' and '11 stone'. One very confused answer in an imperial standard was '7.5 oz'.

David thought the car would be '76 stone 56 kg', Tracy '240 tonnes', Lyne '1 ton' and Yvonne '5 kg 1102 g'.

The majority did not answer any of the parts of this question. The children seemed to be really confused about imperial and metric units. What I need to establish are suitable references for each of the units. We must plan what to teach in weight very carefully to help the children with the different units and 'real' examples.

12 The words beginning with 'a' were mainly 'add' or 'addition'. No one came up with a mathematics word beginning with 'b' (I had thought of 'breadth'). And 'calculate' was the most popular answer for 'c'.

13 Only two children were able to write two further numbers which continued the pattern, Yvonne and David.

Yvonne, probably because she has difficulty with language, either didn't understand the part of the question asking for an explanation of how she found the numbers, or couldn't explain. David's explanation, 'I doubled them all the time', makes no mention of the fact he also had to follow the doubling by adding on one.

14 Only Tracy managed to fill in the boxes with suitable numbers. She completed the first example as $12 \div 2 - 0 = 6$. She made a slip in the second by writing 7 instead of 2, $14 \div 7 - 1 = 6$.

Overall comment

The test gave the children the opportunity to use numbers and write about them. Tracy, David and Lyne gave the 'best' answers among the 11-year-olds, with Linda and Donna leading the way among the younger children. These younger children did well but found the last three parts of question 10 and all the questions which followed very difficult and had little or no success with them. This does indicate that the more difficult questions were towards the end of the test. A few of the children, including Donna, would have liked more time but would have been unlikely to have had greater success.

The test was better suited to the older children, but that may always happen when their greater experience of life and school is an important factor in problem solving.

The test was very revealing for future teaching. I think I shall pin up the test and this analysis of the answers on the staff notice board. I'm sure it will make us think differently about how and what we teach in weight and volume.

Assessment activities

These were only attempted by the children who had the best written results.

Activity A

David, Lyne and Tracy were the three children who found numbers which divided exactly by 13. David found 169, Tracy found 117 and Lyne gave the first number greater than 100, i.e. 104.

Activity B

This proved very difficult. Most of the children tried to describe prisms in terms of corners and sides. For example, Tracy wrote:

> A prism is a shape. It has eight corners. It has six sides to it. Four sides are the same, two sides are not.

She was describing the cuboid. If she had emphasised that all the prisms have two end faces the same, she might have been led into thinking of them being built up from slices all of the same shape and size.

David's description was: 'I think a prism is a sort of diamond shape.' He then wrote for his second attempt, 'A prism is a sort of rectangle.' Perhaps he was realising that most prisms have some rectangular faces and that the cylinder's curved face can be made from a rectangle.

Activity C

This particular program is the last of a sequence of programs about two-dimensional shapes. The children were tackling *Draw a Shape* without any of the experience developed from the earlier programs. They had to choose a shape from a given selection, then draw it on a grid by moving the cursor. They had the choice of choosing 'easy' or 'difficult' shapes. The program gives a score and an average; for example, David scored 10 in 3 shots with an average of 3.3, Tracy scored 7 in 3 shots with an average of 2.3, and Lyne scored 10 in 4 shots and had an average of 3.2.

Overall comment on the activities

David and Tracy both showed systematic working habits. Tracy seems to really enjoy doing the activities. David probably does too but he doesn't show it so obviously.

Structured observation and listening

The children worked in small groups to solve the problem. Most achieved all the problem-solving behaviours stated on the list. They co-operated well and discussed sensibly, with one member adopting the role of recorder naturally. The children did not produce a table of facts reference as had been expected. All three groups produced what might be called a list of hints and an exemplar with huge numbers!

I shall ask each group to present their 'card' to a younger child who does have difficulty with multiplication facts and see what happens.

Overall comment on the observation

David and Tracy who are the two most likely candidates for the course after the activities, worked together on the problem. Tracy found it easier to express her ideas and made a more deliberate effort to listen to David and incorporate what he said. Tracy recorded their ideas like this:

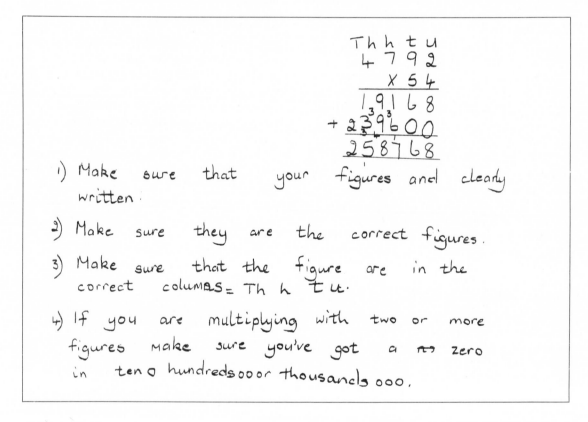

Final choice

The child chosen for the computer course is Tracy.

Example 4

It has been decided that your school should participate in a programme of road safety and issue a local road safety certificate.

The teacher on the committee is asked to draw up the programme for the award of the certificate.

Classification of assessment

The focus of assessment would be on the *ability to apply concepts to a given situation* and *problem solving*.

The children will be assessed on their awareness of road safety as indicated by their decisions about when and where to walk as they travel through neighbourhood streets and in a simulated situation.

Principles of assessment

The summative evaluation would be *criterion referenced*.

Technique of assessment

The technique would be *structured observation*.

Form of assessment

The form could be *assessment activities*.

The first decision to be made is selecting the children to be assessed. In some small schools it could be every child. However, in most, to be manageable, one or two age groups could be considered. For example, a school could decide to assess all children in their first year and all the children in their last year of schooling. This pattern of assessment could be repeated each year.

Most of these practical activities would take place in the community and be observed by a parent or another adult.

The school would set up a simulation in the playground and/or the street outside. Schools often find that the police or the local authority are happy to discuss an event like this and help organise and run it.

Each of the younger children could be given a number of activities to be carried out. Each of these could be watched by an adult who signs a slip of paper to acknowledge that the task has been carried out with an awareness of road safety.

For the school activity, the playground would be set out with chalk-drawn pavements, roads and crossings. Other children would be asked to ride bicycles, drive make-believe cars and be pedestrians. The children to be assessed would be shown the simulated streets, then released from class, one at a time, with the task of taking a message from the school building through the simulated streets to some other point – for example, the janitor's house. One or two observers (parents, older children or teachers) would write a comment on each child's awareness of road safety.

The activity for the older children would involve similar elements. They could be asked to make two specific journeys in the community that involve crossing several roads. Other tasks would involve helping an elderly or blind person across a road, and teaching a 5-year-old how to cross the road. The ability to ride a bicycle (provided by the school) might be an additional optional task depending on the suitability of this for the school's neighbourhood.

The assessment tasks

The Parent Teacher Association committee had organised a meeting to explain to the parents of the selected age groups what was to happen and how they could help.

The school planned the test in parts. The following description concentrates on one part of each test.

1

Name   Age

was able to

cross the road where the Lollipop Man was there to help.

Signed   Date

2

Name   Age

was able to

cross the street at the traffic lights, or a pedestrian

crossing.

Signed   Date

3

Name   Age

was able to

cross the street where there were parked cars.

Signed   Date

4

Name   Age

was able to

go from the house to the school being careful to watch

out for traffic.

Signed   Date

52

The oldest primary class

The specialist teacher for children with learning difficulties reorganised her work for one morning to help the class teacher with this assessment. The task for each child was:

> You are to teach a P1 child the correct way to cross the road.

The two teachers shared the assessment, with one of them observing five children, one after the other, while the other was with the rest of the class, then changing over. This procedure was repeated until all the children had been assessed. Each child went to the infant class to collect his or her 'pupil'. The pair made their way to the road just outside the school gate where the observed 'lesson' took place.

The youngest class

This assessment followed the assessment with the oldest class, and took place after the visit of the community policeman who told the children about road safety.

The forms on page 52 were issued to groups of children over a period of two weeks, so that only a few children were doing each activity at a time. It was possible then for the Lollipop Man to participate as the adult to sign Form 1. Care was taken not to distract him from his road duties.

The school had made it known at the PTA meeting that if it was not possible for a member of the child's family to carry out the task, selected crossing places would be manned by an observer at a specified time to carry out the assessment. These observers were parents from the PTA committee. This message was repeated in a circular sent out with the first form.

The teacher's evaluation of the children's responses

The oldest class

The two teachers involved had discussed together what they hoped would happen, for example:

- there would be an explanation like 'I'm going to teach you how to cross the road';
- a suitable place to cross would be selected with an explanation for this choice;
- the place to stand would be commented on;
- the procedure, 'Look right, look left, look right again' would be shown and explained;
- the child would be reminded to begin the procedure again if traffic was coming;
- the procedure would be carried out quite quickly;
- the child would be reminded to continue to look in both directions as he or she walked across the road.

Rather than tick a checklist, the teachers wrote a few comments. Here are three of these:

Yvonne

On the way through the playground, Yvonne saw a van coming from the kitchen entrance, so she began her 'lesson' with Samantha right away by making us stop and wait until the van passed.

Yvonne chose a position away from parked cars and not too near a corner. She is muddled about naming the directions, but more importantly about the sequence. She suggested left, right, left, so that Samantha could have stepped off the pavement without a final look in the direction of the traffic. Yvonne took Samantha across the road once in each direction and then let her try crossing by herself. Samantha's eyes were on Yvonne as she crossed the road, not the traffic. Yvonne told her she had to 'Listen, look and think' and she tapped her head on this last word to try to explain what she meant.

It was important that Samantha did not learn the 'look' procedure wrongly. The sequence of directions was discussed with Yvonne explaining why it was important that the right, the direction of the traffic, should be the final direction. She then went over this with Samantha.

Yvonne was very protective on the way back to the school gate, placing Samantha on her inner side, away from the traffic.

Michael

Michael found it difficult to shepherd young Andrew around. He did not take his hand as one of the girls would have done but rather left Andrew to follow him.

Michael chose a suitable spot and taught Andrew where to look by putting his hands on Andrew's head and twisting it in the appropriate directions as he said, 'Look this way, then this way'. He directed Andrew to look right, then left, then 'up there' – to a road opposite where traffic was likely to come from. Having shown Andrew what to do, he questioned him, 'What do you do first? What do you do second?' Andrew found this difficult to follow. Michael asked him if he knew the Green Cross Code and was horrified when Andrew shook his head. He asked Andrew if he knew what a zebra crossing was. On discovering that Andrew didn't know this either, he tried to show him that it was black and white lines on the road. This demonstration took him out on to the road! Michael was worried to find out that Andrew's older brother brings him to school and that he runs across the roads.

George

Here is what happened in this instance.

GEORGE: Right, stand there. Right. I'm going to teach you to cross the road.
Look that way (*Points left*).
Right, look that way (*Points right*).
Right, walk.
Keep looking.
DEBRA: (*No spoken response – very shy.*)

The above was repeated more or less the same three times altogether. George showed no awareness of the Green Cross Code. He looked left before right. He did not mention listening for traffic. He showed a very kindly attitude to Debra but no real sense of responsibility for her.

Overall comment

This activity gave us feedback on which children

- know the correct 'looking' sequence,
- can explain this,
- consider appropriate language for 5-year-olds,
- are aware of other aspects of road safety.

We would add to our original list of points to look for and would teach road safety quite differently now. It seems we have been emphasising what to do and neglecting to explain why these actions should be taken.

The youngest children

The Lollipop Man had attended the PTA meeting. This assessment task seems to have given him a new dimension to his job. He does not just shepherd the children across the road now but explains why he can't let them cross and why he can. As he waits with the young children he talks aloud; for example, 'We can't stop the traffic just now because there is too much of it. Look how close that car is behind the red one. We couldn't get between them. Look, after the blue car, there is a gap. What about the other way? Good, there is a gap among the cars that way too. Right, another look this way. I'll step out to hold up my sign, then I'll tell you to cross.'

He greatly enjoyed observing the children's behaviour as they waited on the pavement and then as they crossed the road. He signed the forms, often writing a comment as well: for example, 'Marianne watches the traffic as she crosses.'

It was found that the parents, too, like to add comments, sometimes about which road was crossed, the traffic conditions, and what the child did well. A section for such comments could be included on the forms next year.

Overall comment

I have gained a great deal through this

assessment, particularly by working with the parents and the Lollipop Man. I have met some of the children's families for the first time, and had a sense of sharing concern about the child with them. This will help me to approach them – and hopefully help them to approach me – in the future.

Example 5

The school has decided to move to an assessment policy which does not assess individual subjects but instead emphasises an across-the-curriculum approach. The teacher of the top primary class has been asked to suggest how 'language across the curriculum' can be assessed in her class.

Classification of assessment

The focus of assessment is on *communication*.

The children are required to show that they can communicate in writing, by drawing and by talking. In each instance what is being communicated has a subject context other than 'language', and often draws on several aspects of the curriculum.

Principles of assessment

The assessment should be *formative* and *criterion referenced*.

Techniques of assessment

The techniques which could be adopted are

- *writing*,
- *practical activity*, and
- *structured observation and listening.*

Form of assessment

The forms of assessment to be used could be pretending to be a character from a novel or project and writing a letter; drawing a map; talking on tape; talking to an adult; participating in a group discussion to solve a problem.

All the children should be involved in all these tasks. The writing of the letter and drawing of the map can be carried out by a large group unsupervised. Talking on tape can be carried out by the children working individually unsupervised, possibly in the corridor, in the open area, or in another room. Talking to an adult should be carried out by individuals talking to the class teacher or another member of staff. The problem-solving groups need to be monitored by a teacher but only for a short time. There is no need to listen to the full discussion.

This mixture of assessment procedures can run smoothly if the teacher divides the class into three groups and engages each in a different form of assessment, as shown in the example below:

Group 1	Group 2	Group 3
letter	problem solving	map drawing with talking on tape
problem solving	map drawing with talking on tape	letter
map drawing with talking on tape	letter	problem solving

Later, each child should talk to an adult, withdrawing the children from class one by one. A colleague could help with this by supervising the rest of the class.

The assessment tasks

Writing

Task 1   The Letter: Here is an example based on the children's study of the book *Mouldy's Orphans*. The instructions to the children were:

> Pretend to be either Mouldy or Billy.
> Write a letter to someone.

The children were asked to be one of two selected people, a man and a woman. Most boys choose to be the male character, Billy, and most girls choose to be Mouldy.

The children chose for themselves the person they would write to and what they should write about. However, the teacher discussed this with one or two children to help them attempt the task.

The children can be given sheets of paper to fold and put in an envelope. In other instances it may be more appropriate to ask the children to roll up their sheets and tie it with ribbon.

Task 2   The Map: The instruction, used by a school where all the children live in nearby houses, was:

> Draw a map showing your home, the streets you come along on your way to school, and the school.

The children were given a sheet of plain A4 size paper.

Assessment activities

Activity A   Talking on tape

Instruction card
Choose one of the shapes.
Tell the tape recorder your name.
Now, without saying the name of the shape, describe it as fully as you can so that classmates can guess which is your shape.

Materials
Five three-dimensional shapes: for ex-ample, a triangular pyramid, a cone, a hexagonal prism, a cylinder, and an octahedron. These should be of different colours so that the children can name them by colour. Strips of paper and a pencil, as well as a box with the instructions 'Post your paper here' on it. A tape recorder, loaded with a blank tape, should have the 'play', 'record' and 'pause' buttons depressed.

While drawing the map in Task 2, the children followed one another in turn to carry out this talking activity. The tape recorder was placed in an empty room next door, where the child was undisturbed. Supervision was not necessary.

The completed tape was played to the class so that the teacher could consider each child's fluency, ability to organise the description and the use of mathematical vocabulary. The interest shown and the naming of the shape by the children in the class was used as an element of the teacher's evaluation. Listening to the descriptions took place over two short sessions rather than one long one.

Activity B   Using a map

Instruction card
Show Mrs Davenport the way you come to school on your map. Tell her what you see and do on the journey.

Materials
Each child uses his or her own map. The adult considers the child's fluency and knowledge of the area as well as the support gained from using the map.

Problem solving

The children worked in groups of three. They were given a 'real' problem to discuss and to try to resolve:

> Discuss the ways in which school dinners could be better.

You might talk about what you get to eat, and how it is served.

When you are ready, make a list of things you all think should be changed.

Only one sheet of paper and one pencil was supplied so that the children should work together.

The teacher who monitored the group discussions completed this checklist for each child:

Children's Names

The child		
1 joins in the discussion		
2 does not monopolise the conversation		
3 gives reasoned opinions about the ideas of others		
4 can express an idea or opinion effectively		

A few children's responses and the teacher's evaluation

Written communication

1 The letter (*Mouldy's Orphans*)
Here are three of the letters.

Canal Row
OX Ford shire

Dear Mr Gerald

Our sister mouldy has found a poor orphan boy called Benjy she found him at the trian station when she came home from the Ferter she took him home to get something to eat she said to her mum and dad can he stay to night my mum siad yes but in the morning he must go to the Vicarich

yours Billy K

Canal Row
Oxfordshire.

Dear Tracy McBain,
How are you. I am not
to well at the moment. I went to the Panto
Last night and it was very good. I mett
a boy called Benjy and I brought him home
I thought the children would welcome him
but it was only my mum and dad who
welomed him into the family. On sunday
we had our lunch mum gave benjy some food
too. May had to sit on my knee so that
Benjy could have her seat he did not know
how to use the Crokery so he eat with
his fingers. Mum said to dad if that
was any of our children they would have
got a sore back-side but it was not.
Then Dad said he will have to go to the
Work-shed but I. said no they treat
you like slaves in that place. You get out
once a year. You don't get feed well enough.
So mum said we shall take him to the
Vicarage. The vicarea said we shall take him
Then we will take him to Oxford. We
know of a boy's home there. and they will
be good to him they said I could go along to. So they
took him and when I. came home I
was very pleased that he got a nice
home to live. Well see you tommorow
at school Tracy.
From
Mouldy Kippers.

58

> Canal Row
> Oxfordshire
>
> Dear Mr Gerald,
>   It was a lovely pantomime.
> I met a friend Benjy he's an orphan. I told
> him to go home with me I said he'd be
> loved for and cared for. But he has to
> go back to the out skirts of Oxfordshire
> to a house where he works and has
> all his hair cut of and they
> all were the same clothes and
> nobody will love him. The vicor
> said I could go to Oxfordshire when
> he is leaving. Bye.
>
>   Your trully
>   Mouldy Kippers.

Most children wrote to Mr Gerald, a character in the book, or to a classmate. When I commented about the suitability of a classmate, the children assured me that the children in the story went to school and had friends who could have had these names!

Some of the children became so involved in the task that the layout for writing a letter was forgotten, while others put in the fictional address and began 'Dear _____' in the usual way. Only two children signed the letter with their own name, forgetting to use their fictional name.

The amount of the story which came into their letters varied greatly. There were instances of the present being confused with the past; for example, 'He might take us to the pantomime again to see another film'. It will be interesting to follow this up to find out if it was just a slip or a misunderstanding of what a pantomime is.

I would certainly use this format again because the children were considering the novel in a quite different way as they tried to adopt their chosen character's viewpoint.

2 The map, from house to school –
Although some of the children used the accepted rectangles for buildings, most labelled these and/or still had one building drawn in elevation – usually their own house. Many had all buildings drawn in elevation. The children obviously feel that their attempts at formal map representations may be misunderstood and want to overcome this. I am reminded of the fact that many tourist maps have historic buildings and landmarks as elevations because they are either familiar in that form or can be emphasised in this way. I don't intend to comment to the children on this at the moment. It is more important, I think, for them to plan the area to be shown more effectively on the page. Yvonne's map will be a good discussion point here. She has part of the map on one side of the sheet and part on the other side!

Yvonne's map drawn on two sides of the sheet of paper

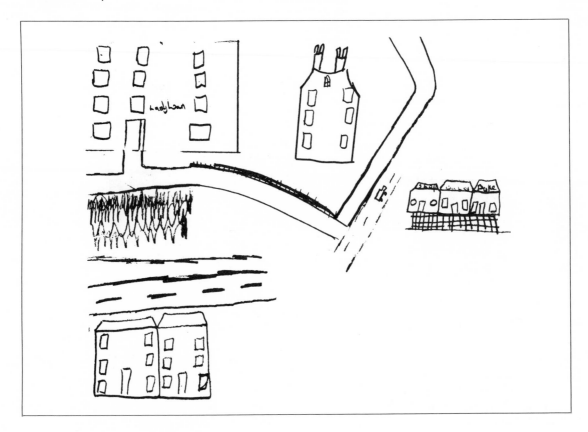

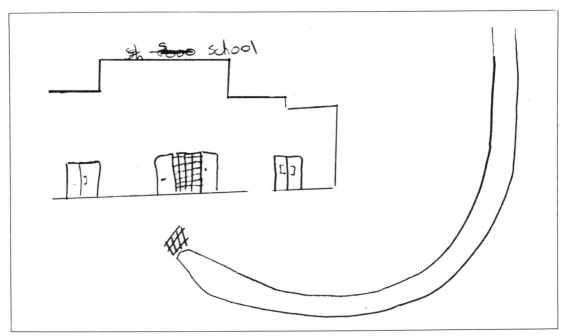

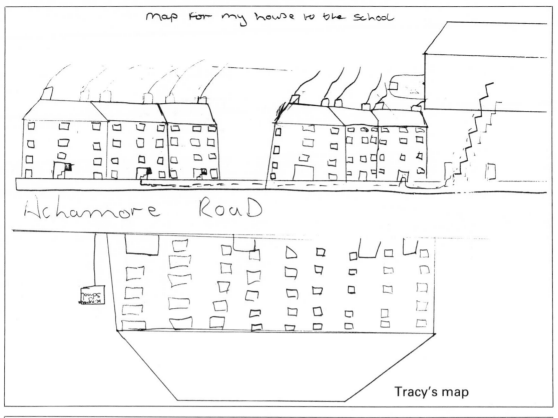

map for my house to the school

Achamore Road

Tracy's map

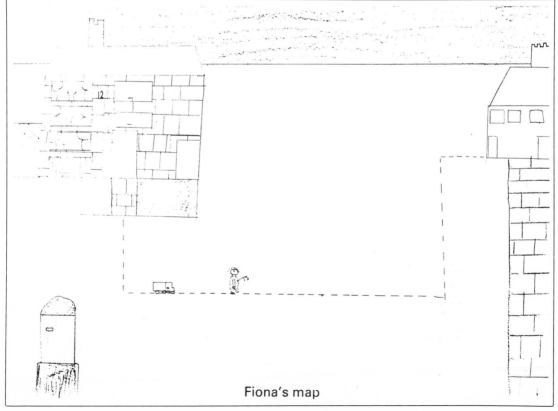

Fiona's map

First attempt (uncompleted)

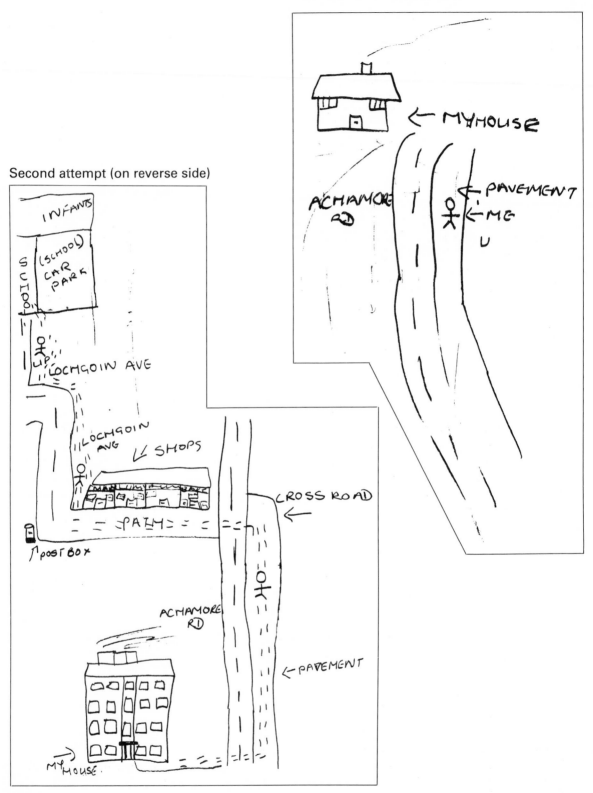

Second attempt (on reverse side)

62

When children are asked to draw a map, it should be for a specific purpose. One of the most common purposes is to tell someone the route from one place to another. Tracy shows her route to school with the landmarks of a friend's house and steps. Such landmarks are missing in Fiona's map, although there is the pillar box down in the left-hand corner.

Both of these maps could be the focus of a discussion about what should be the important features of a map. Is it curtains, cars, smoke from the chimneys, pillar boxes and bus stops? Or is it named roads, approximate distances, directions and buildings at corners? This would enable the girls and others to build on what they are doing at present.

The map on page 62 began with 'my house' near the top of the page. However, a second version with 'my house' at the foot of the page followed on the reverse of the sheet. This change of thought will make an interesting discussion point on how to begin by placing the two named buildings on the sheet and considering approximate directions and distances.

The feedback from this assessment and from the descriptions using the maps (Activity B) will provide exemplars for me to help the children. I am keeping one or two maps for each mixed-ability group and will use them when we go outside to look more closely at features in the neighbourhood.

Assessment activities

Activity A Talking on tape

The children enjoyed this activity. Although the tape recorder was set so that only the 'pause' button was to be used, some of the children wished to re-record their description. I let them do this.

Their descriptions allowed me to make sets of word cards. One set was of words which were used to mean different things – for example, 'side' was used for the flat or curved face of a shape and also used for the edge where two faces meet. Other words like this

were 'long' and 'round'. Another set contained specific words like 'rectangle' and 'longer'. A third set had descriptive phrases like 'a witch's hat'.

Because the descriptions were detailed and included colour, most of the shapes were easily identified. However, the children had no doubts about what were 'good clues', and they soon realised that order was important and began to suggest that one sentence should have come before another. If anyone said the name of the shape by mistake, the class was bitterly disappointed at being deprived of guessing.

The children need more practice in thinking about the most appropriate words to use and in giving descriptions on tape. I can see many possibilities in science and local area studies as well as music and art, where I can give the children something to describe.

Activity B Using your map

David's map is shown on p. 64. Here are Mrs Davenport's notes on his description of the route.

David had great difficulty in getting started with his description. He did not use his map to help him explain. He had difficulty in talking in sentences at the beginning but this improved as he gained confidence. The detail of the route was interesting.

ME: Tell me how you go to school.
DAVID: I go two ways.
ME: Tell me the shortest way.
DAVID: Ladyloan Road, the rocky path, then down twenty-four steps. Then cross over Lochgoin Road, then go down the pavement. Then turn left and in at the gate. Then in and down another twelve stairs, and that's me in school.

The comments below relate to Fiona's map shown on page 61.

Fiona used the second person to describe her route. She did not use the map or point out the route.

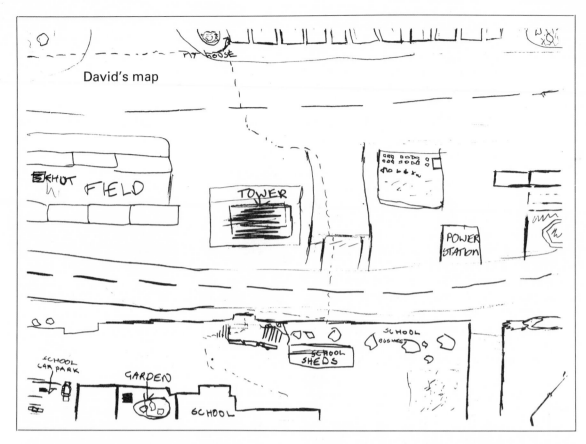

David's map

You come out of the door at the close. Then you go down the steps and you turn the corner. You go straight down Ladyloan Avenue. You are at the bottom of Ladyloan Avenue. Then you turn the corner and go up, and then you cross the road and go into the school.

Fiona had put the house number very high on the building. I wondered if this was because she lived on the top floor, and I asked her to show me the windows of her house, but they were on the ground floor.

provided. The headteacher agreed that this would be an improvement. She was aware of the need for water being served but the meals service would not accept the extra work involved in washing tumblers. As the head looked at one group's list, she noted they had written that they would like milk to drink. She asked why they wanted milk: 'Because we can keep it from break and drink it with our dinner.' The problem was solved!

Some extracts from the children's lists are shown on pages 65 and 66.

Problem solving

This assessment became much more than information on an individual's effectiveness in discussion. The children listed sensible improvements for the school dinners. For example, every group requested that a drink be

Overall comment

There is little doubt that I have a great deal to note about each child's communication skills. A child's ability to communicate in writing was often at a different standard from his or her oral and diagrammatic communication skills.

change The prayers
change The runny custerd into thick custerd
cut the fatnes out of the meat
The potaos are to dry So they Should give out drinks
The teAtchers should eAt in the Dinner HALL too.

You should change The tAbles about

The cutlery Should not be durty. And bent

They should change The Pottatos to chips

And the should not give extras.

The dinner ladey shoud not (Shout) at use
They Should give out fresh frute

The Diner Lady should not tell you what to do.

you shoud be aloud to Sit   were ever you want
        Ross   Margiet   michael
        Tom   Ross   Beacham
                          Rose
                          kirkwood

School dinners

1.) WE should be Given more choices. keep it for lunch
2.) WE should get milk with our dinner. *
3.) we should get salt pepper vinyor and sauce.
4.) the cutlery should not be bent.
5.) we 'should' get more choices of puddin's.
6.) we should get our dinner at 12.30 Exactolly.
7.) we Should get chair's at the table.
8.) we don't get BEEtroot and colesaw much.
9.) we don't Get chips so offen.
10.) we should get more dinner people.

×) From ALISON C
        Anbrea
           oneill
              RAB

Tracy M (School Meals)
+ +
Susan S

1) We should get drinks with Our dinner.

2) We should get Salt and Sauce.

3) We should get 3 choices

4) We should be in for twelve thirty on the dot

5) If you are late for dinner you should get a note

6)

David is an example here. He is much better at communicating in writing, both words and drawings, than he is orally. The tape recorder seemed to help him because no one else was there. Talking about his map and in the group discussion he appeared tongue-tied and hesitant. He'll need help in such situations, although more practice may be the greatest need.

I intend to ask parents to provide a cassette tape. I'll let each child use their own tape when talking and describing. I'll keep this in their folders of work. Towards the end of the session, we'll play extracts from the beginning and from the end, and see if fluency and vocabulary are improved. The tape can then be sent to the parents. It would be a good idea to make a tape span several years. I must ask the rest of the staff what they think.

Example 6

As part of the school's assessment policy, it has been agreed that the school will assess attitudes. The teacher has been asked to consider how she would assess the children in her class in their caring attitude towards classmates who are less able mentally or physically than themselves.

Classification of assessment

The focus of assessment would be on *attitudes*.

Principles of assessment

The assessment would be *criterion referenced*.

Technique of assessment

The technique which would be used is *informal observation*. This means that the children would not be aware that they were being assessed – certainly not about their attitudes.

Form of the assessment

In order to assess the children's caring attitude towards the child who is less able physically, it was decided to use a group problem in the gym. There were no physically disabled children in the class. There were, however, children who were less agile and might not participate with ease. It was the other children's caring attitude to these children in their group which was monitored.

The problem given to the class was this:

> Make up exercises which everyone in the class will enjoy doing. They should last no longer than five minutes.

For assessment of the children's caring attitude to those children who are less able mentally, it was decided to use a mathematics dominoes-type game where the children were required to match equivalent vulgar and decimal fractions. The game was new to them, and it was anticipated that most children would find it difficult.

The children worked in mixed ability groups of four. The attitude of the children who mastered the game towards those who found the game difficult was monitored.

The twenty-eight 'dominoes' which were used in the game are shown on page 68.

The teacher decided to use the stages of 'attitude adoption' used earlier in this book, and made a checklist for monitoring each child's attitude like this:

Receiving	The child showed an acknowledgment that others are different from himself or herself and that this difference is a matter of concern.
Responding	The child made this concern explicit in discussion with others.
Valuing	The child demonstrated this concern for the less able classmate, seeking an opinion or a positive suggestion so that the classmate was able to participate.
Organisation by value	The child offered help in a supportive way. (This level is difficult to assess in one lesson because it really requires the child to be monitored over a period of time.)

Where the child was not responding, the teacher had decided to take him or her aside for a few moments so as to discuss if they thought the exercise/game was suitable for everyone in the class and why or why not.

$\frac{1}{2}$	0·5	$\frac{2}{4}$	$\frac{5}{10}$	$\frac{1}{2}$	0·5	$\frac{5}{10}$
$\frac{1}{4}$	$\frac{3}{4}$	$\frac{1}{10}$	1·5	$\frac{4}{2}$	$\frac{1}{3}$	0·3
$\frac{1}{4}$	0·25	$\frac{2}{8}$	$\frac{1}{4}$	0·25	$\frac{1}{4}$	$\frac{1}{3}$
0·75	$\frac{1}{10}$	$\frac{3}{2}$	$\frac{2}{1}$	$\frac{1}{3}$	$\frac{3}{10}$	0·3
$\frac{3}{4}$	0·75	$\frac{3}{4}$	0·75	$\frac{3}{4}$	2	$\frac{2}{4}$
0·1	$1\frac{1}{2}$	2	$\frac{2}{6}$	0·3	$\frac{1}{3}$	$\frac{3}{10}$
$\frac{1}{10}$	0·1	$\frac{10}{100}$	0·1	1·5	$1\frac{1}{2}$	$\frac{3}{2}$
1·5	$\frac{6}{3}$	$\frac{1}{3}$	0·3	2	$\frac{1}{3}$	$\frac{30}{100}$

The set of dominoes is made by cutting along the thick black lines

The teacher's evaluation of some children's responses

At gym

One group consisted of three girls and a boy. One of the girls, Alison, is rather plump. The group began, as did all the groups, with individuals trying to show the others an exercise which might be used. At one point during this 'trying out', the exercise was to lie on your back with hips raised off the floor and legs stretched back so that toes touched the floor behind your head, and Alison said, 'I can't do that'. The others ignored this comment. The actions of the others in this group, and in all the other groups, indicated clearly that they were not 'responding' to those less physically able.

However, what was interesting was the response of the children who were less agile. Alison had to decide what she should do about the exercises she found difficult to perform. She took a very positive approach, and set out to persuade the others to include *her* choice of exercises – which, of course, were ones she could do. The other girls accepted her ideas. I believe this indicates that the girls were at the attitude-adoption level of 'receiving'.

George, a less agile boy in a group of two boys and two girls, reacted differently. He could not carry out the exercises which were chosen by the two girls. When the group were asked to show their exercises to the others, he became the clown carrying out the exercises in an exaggerated manner. I realise that my main criterion for forming the groups was to have a less agile child in each. If George had been with other boys, possibly friends, would he have been able to influence them as Alison had managed to do with the girls in her group? I shall have to try this.

The other interesting attitude which I found myself monitoring, without having intended to do so, was the girls' co-operative attitude to the boys in their group. In Alison's group the three girls tended to ignore the one boy. One of the girls did turn to him on two occasions, and said, 'What do you think, Alec?' I noted that her co-operative attitude to this boy was at the 'responding' level. In George's group the two girls more or less ignored the boys and the boys followed their suggestions. The girls were not at the 'receiving' level in their co-operative attitude to the boys, whereas the boys seemed to be at the 'receiving' level in their co-operative attitude to the girls. This would have to be confirmed through further assessment.

The groups performed energetic sequences of exercises. The others made comments like 'They went too fast' and 'The exercises were too difficult'. Instead of talking to individuals I spoke to the whole class. I reminded them that the exercises were to be enjoyed by everyone, and asked them what they would do about exercises that were too difficult. The majority view was that if anyone could not do them that was 'too bad'. One girl seemed to be at the level of 'receiving' in her caring attitude, and said, 'You shouldn't put in ones people can't do'.

The class assessment of the caring attitude to children less physically able was that the majority had not reached the 'receiving' level. Some children had reached the level of 'responding' and one child had showed evidence of 'valuing'.

The dominoes game

One group was made up of two boys and two girls. One boy, Robert, and one girl, Fiona, found the game more difficult than the others. Fiona kept her dominoes hidden under the table. Robert, realising that he required help, put his dominoes face up on the table for all to see. The others offered no help: this might prevent them winning! If either Robert or Fiona took a long time to play, they were urged to hurry up, or were asked, 'Are you knocking?' To the others' amazement, Fiona won. She had been able to play by merely matching identical fractions. The brighter children were not aware of this because of their own difficulties in identifying equivalent fractions. In a second game, competition was keen and comment more abrasive; for example, 'You don't deal like that', and 'Put it [the first domino] where we can all see it'. The two brighter children were obviously aware that the others were having difficulties. There was no evidence of a caring attitude. There is no evidence that these children had 'received'.

In another group, a girl shouted at the child in difficulty, 'Play point seven five'. This was only to allow the game to continue and is not evidence of caring. In another group, a brighter child leaned forward and played the appropriate domino for a less able player, but only because this allowed her to play. She also showed no evidence of caring. Two children were noted to be 'valuing'. Susan said, 'Put the dominoes in front of you on the table. I'll help you.' Craig also offered help. Both gave the help by making comments like 'You have a domino which fits here. Now look at all your dominoes. What is another way of having a half?' This is only a single incident, so it is not possible to say whether these children have reached the level of 'organisation by value' as this has to be based on a number of observations.

Overall comment

It would seem that the majority of the class, from the evidence of the two assessment tasks, are not at the 'receiving' level in their caring attitude towards those less able than themselves.

This is my first attempt at assessing attitudes. I am not really sure that I understand the different levels as clearly as I would like to. However, I'm aware of the importance of these levels because I realise that the teaching associated with each level will have a different approach.

I have found the assessment extremely interesting and thought-provoking. I would now like to plan some teaching and assessment for the 'receiving' level of the caring attitude, but I'll need help with this. If the head can't help, she will contact the local college of education.

We hope these exercises urge you to try to assess different aspects of the curriculum and to experiment with techniques you have not tried before. It will be most rewarding both for your teaching and for what you find out about the children.

5 Background information

Most books on assessment begin with background information, but we have not used this approach. We suggest you look up the background information when you need it. In this section we explain the following basic ideas of assessment:

- validity,
- reliability,
- objective and subjective, and
- norm-referenced assessment and criterion-referenced assessment.

We also offer explanations of certain terms which are widely used in assessment:

- 'diagnostic'   • 'power test'
- 'formative'   • 'self-reference'
- 'halo effect'   • 'summative'

We offer explanations of some terms which we have used in our analysis and printed in bold face in this book:

- 'concept'   • 'skill'
- 'principle'   • 'prompt'

For a teacher, a 'valid' and 'reliable' assessment item represents the practical manifestation of a curricular intention. What do we mean by these terms?

Validity

A test is valid in so far as it measures what it claims to measure.

In the primary school it is very difficult to produce a test which is 100 per cent valid – that is, it measures only what it purports to measure. For example, written tests in mathematics involve:

- reading,
- interpretation,
- knowledge of a variety of concepts and skills,
- ability to apply this knowledge, and
- recording the answer.

If the teacher is assured that a particular test item is valid, then the teacher can assume that it measures what it purports to measure – that is, that it measures the curriculum intention. The teacher has a teaching objective.

Tips for deciding whether a test is valid or not:

1 Is there adequate identification of the objectives to be assessed by the test? If not, analyse what objectives the test *does* measure, and decide if these are adequate.
2 Is there to be a clear relationship between the individual items in the test and the objectives of the course?
3 Is there a structure for working, and does

this structure relate to the objectives of the course?

Reliability

A test is reliable (stable) in so far as it is immune from chance influences and gives consistent results in what it does measure.

Tips for improving the reliability of your assessment:

1 the more questions you use to cover a topic, the more reliable is the coverage;
2 re-marking improves reliability;
3 the use of a marking scheme based on a structured analysis of the task also improves reliability (as we suggest on p. 33, for example).

Objective and subjective

Many of the everyday classroom exercises that are set by primary teachers for their pupils are objective – for example, in computation and spelling. A question is objective when the answer is independent of the teacher's judgement. By implication, a question is subjective when the correctness of the answer is determined by the teacher's judgement.

Subjectivity is a matter of degree rather than of level. Consider these questions:

1 Which 3-D shape has six identical square faces?
2 Which word is the opposite of happy?
3 Re-write this sentence placing the word 'curious' in the best position. 'The cat seemed to give a smile.'
4 What 3-D shape has six faces?
5 What word means not happy?
6 Write a sentence with the word 'curious' in it.
7 Describe a 3-D shape.
8 Give an adjective which describes how the girl was feeling.
9 Make up a story about a curious happening.

These questions are progressively more open. The more open the question, the more freedom is given to the child; the greater the divergence of assessments by different teachers, the more subjective are those assessments.

When questions are more specific, and if marking schemes are used, objectivity in marking is increased and assessment becomes more reliable.

Norm-referenced assessment and criterion-referenced assessment

Below is a conversation from a secondary school staffroom:

JOHN: That was a poor question you set in the second-year maths paper, Bill.
BILL: Why, what was wrong with it?
JOHN: It was too difficult – none of the pupils could do it. . . And while I'm at it, yours wasn't much better, Peter, it was too easy – they could all do it!

Implication: a good question is a question that some pupils get right and some pupils get wrong.

This is only true for a norm-referenced test. The Moray House tests (AQs, EQs and VRQs) were norm-referenced tests. They were popular in primary schools twenty years ago. Most of you will be too young to remember them in schools, although some of you might have taken them as pupils.

Norm-referenced tests emphasise differences between individual children; they put children in an order of merit. The purpose of the test is to indicate relative levels of performance.

A criterion-referenced test places the emphasis on absolute levels of performance. This usually involves checking that what has been taught has indeed been learned. If pupils reach the standard, they are deemed satisfactory, and if they do not reach the standard, then they are deemed unsatisfactory.

A good question is one which tests the absolute performance. If all pupils reach the standard, give yourself a pat on the back – there can be nothing wrong with the question. If all the pupils get it wrong, it may still not be the fault of the question, and perhaps what you should be doing is looking again at your teaching.

Formative and summative assessment

Much of the assessment in the primary classroom is formative assessment: assessment concerned with providing information for class management decisions. It is concerned with decisions about adapting the day-to-day classroom provision to the class, the group or the individual. It is concerned with improving provision, and about decisions about moving on and to what topic. Currently much formative assessment in the primary school is informal and is done by observation. The results are not usually recorded. The assessment takes place in the day-to-day work of the class. We suggest that more formative assessment should be recorded.

The counterpoint to formative assessment is summative assessment. In summative assessment the concern is a final assessment, a final judgement about a course or a class or an individual child.

The summative assessment takes place at the end of a course, a term or a unit. Summative assessments are usually formal, an end of topic assessment.

However, summative assessments need not be formal in that the final judgement can be based on impressions gained throughout the term or the year (sometimes called continuous assessment). Such assessments tend to be less reliable.

Diagnostic assessment

In diagnostic assessment we try to pinpoint exactly what the child can and cannot do with a view to identifying an individual child's difficulty and providing appropriate remediation.

Diagnostic assessment is a worthwhile activity but has limitations. The assessment procedures themselves have to be fairly extensive and thorough, in order to pinpoint difficulties. Some of the difficulties identified do not lend themselves to remediation.

Halo effect

The bias in assessment which reflects personal values is called the 'halo effect', particularly when it reflects what we like and admire. It is one source of divergence between the assessments of two teachers looking at the same piece of work. Cross-marking, or discussing a piece of work with a colleague, can highlight the effect, and enable allowance to be made for it.

Item bank

This is a bank of questions, usually MCQs, available for selection by individual teachers. Items in any bank have usually been extensively piloted, and they are often supported by statistical data on the difficulty of individual items. The statistical data are norm-referenced, and are of dubious value if you are selecting items for a criterion-referenced test.

In the seventies item banks were seen as a pool of material to be tapped by an individual teacher. They have not been so prominent in the eighties, perhaps because of some questioning of the assumption which lay behind the criteria for determining the difficulty of an item.

Power test

Power tests are used in normative assessment, when our intention is to put children in an order of merit. Perhaps we want to assess the best (or the worst). Our concern is not absolute standards but relative standards of those taking the test – who is better than whom.

One way of doing this is to arrange that the questions in the test are progressively more difficult and put a quite severe time limit on the test, so that few, if any, children will finish all the questions. This is called a power test. The old 12-plus selective tests (including AQ, EQ and VRQ tests) were all power tests.

(In SRA reading kits there are 'power tests'. Technically they are misnamed. The objective is to have the child read a few paragraphs, then answer some MCQs, and to do this quickly. The criterion is speed. They are criterion-referenced tests.)

Self-reference

This is a name given to the assessment process where a child's achievement is compared with his achievement in the past – say, three months, six months and one year ago. The focus is the development of the individual child.

Concept

An important human capability is to put things into a class and respond to the class as a whole. For example, *cat, chair, tree, house* are known as concrete concepts. They can be denoted by pointing to them – concepts of observation.

Other concepts are abstract in the sense that they involve relations – *happiness, early, brave, assessment, evaluation*. There are also concepts of definition – *odd, edge, diagonal, square root, subject, object*.

Principle

Technically a principle or rule is an inferred capability that enables the individual to respond to a class of situations with a class of performances. They are chains of concepts.

For example, the individual child could respond to the class of situations:

$$2 + 3, 3 + 4, 7 + 5 \text{ and so on}$$
with $3 + 2, 4 + 3, 5 + 7$

In other words, there is a principle that adding numbers is not dependent on the order of the numbers which are to be combined.

Examples of rules:

round things roll,
metamorphosis occurs when the larvae of an insect turns to a pupa,
birds fly,
in Scotland some birds fly south in winter.

Prompt

In the context of assessment a prompt is additional help given to the child to answer a direct question. Most prompts are formal prompts, giving a clue to the form of the answer, perhaps by indicating the number of words required for the answer by a series of dashes, perhaps giving the first letter of a word or writing in the unit of the answer.

While prompts may be an appropriate part of a teaching sequence, we would have to seriously question their use in assessment.

Skill

A skill can be explained as something the child learns to do. Some educationists consider skills can be acquired by rote learning and the child performs them without understanding. An example often quoted is computation in mathematics. However, the term 'skill' is used in contexts where understanding and thinking are part of the action performed by the child. Manipulative skills can range from tying shoelaces to preparing a page layout. Environmental studies use the term 'skill' to 'include both the development of practical abilities and the development of attitudes' (*Environmental Studies in the Primary School*, SCES).

This means that the term 'skill' is used to

represent a very wide range of different interpretations. Even a dictionary doesn't help:

> skill – knowledge of any art or science and dexterity in the practice of it; expertness.

Our advice is to think much more about what you mean and use a more appropriate term.

Postscript

As you work through the book applying some of the ideas to your own situation, perhaps you will have decided that assessment solves some problems but leads to others. We agree. Two examples illustrate this.

On pages 67 to 70 we describe a series of steps in the assessment of attitudes. In our illustration, the attitude was that the children should have a caring attitude towards those less fortunate than themselves mentally or physically. We piloted our suggestions in local schools. One school has discovered that the children have not developed this attitude. The school wants to do something about it, and the question is how!

In another school we piloted assessment items on practical mathematics. The teachers believed that they had covered this work. We drew a sample from three classes. The pupils did not do well. We continued developing our materials and went back to pilot them with a second sample from the same classes. This time the pupils did very well. Was this because our materials were so much better? We were not so naïve as to believe so. After our first visit, the teachers had realised the children's misconceptions and had gone on to make sure that their pupils could undertake the practical tasks.

These two examples illustrate the general principle that, besides measuring, assessment can and does exert a powerful influence on teaching (and on learning). There is a lesson here for curricular development in the primary school. If something is built into the assessment system, then surely it will be taught. This principle we call 'assessment-led curriculum development' and, in our view, it is a very powerful tool for curriculum change.

References

KRATHWOHL, D. R., BLOOM, B. S. and MASIA, B. B. (1964) *Taxonomy of Educational Objectives. Handbook II: Affective Domain.* Harlow: Longman.

LEVY, P. and GOLDSTEIN, H. (1984) *Tests in Education: A Book of Critical Reviews.* London: Academic Press.

Sources of useful information

Assessment of Performance Unit (APU) (1980) *Mathematical Development, Primary School Survey 1.* London: HMSO.

Assessment of Performance Unit (APU) (1981) *Mathematical Development, Primary School Survey 2.* London: HMSO.

Assessment of Performance Unit (APU) (1981) *Science in Schools, Age 11: Report No. 1.* London: HMSO.

Assessment of Performance Unit (APU) (1981) *Language Performance in Schools, Primary School Report 1.* London: HMSO.

Assessment of Performance Unit (APU) (1982) *Mathematical Development, Primary School Survey 3.* London: HMSO.

Assessment of Performance Unit (APU) (1982) *Language Performance in Schools, Primary School Report 2.* London: HMSO.

DUNCAN. A. and MITCHELL, L. (1986) *Assessment Activities in Mathematics.* Jordanhill College of Education Learning Resources, Glasgow.

DUNCAN, A., DUNDAS, K., HENDERSON, N. and MORRIS, A. (1987) *We've Done It.* A Series of Starter Packs for Problem Solving. Aylesbury: Ginn and Co.

Department of Education and Science (DES) Reports

DES (1978) *Primary Education in England.* London: HMSO.

DES (1982) *Education 5 to 9.* London: HMSO.

Acknowledgments

The authors would especially like to acknowledge the contribution from participants in the National course 'Assessment in the Primary School' sponsored by the Scottish Education Department whose comments were helpful in the drafting of this book.

They would also like to acknowledge the contribution from the staff and children of Lochgoin Primary School, Drumchapel, Glasgow, who willingly participated in the development of material for this book and to so many of the projects.

The authors and publishers would like to thank the following for permission to use material in this book:
Jordanhill College of Education for the extract on p. 29 taken from A. Duncan and L. Mitchell (1986) *Assessment Activities in Mathematics*; NFER-Nelson for the extract on p. 24 taken from R. Fyfe and E. Mitchell (1985) *Reading Strategies and Their Assessment*; Ginn & Company Ltd for the extract on p. 33 taken from A. Duncan, K. Dundas, N. Henderson and A. Morris (1987) *We've Done It!*; Heinemann Educational Books Ltd for the extract on p. 23 taken from the Scottish Primary Mathematics Group, Stage 4 (1986) *Primary Mathematics: A Development Through Activity*; The Controller of HMSO for the extracts on pp. 21, 22, 23, 24, 27, 29 and 30. Cover photo taken by Brian Lochrin.

Index